# THE JOURNEY

by the author of STRANGE FRUIT

and KILLERS OF THE DREAM

---

# LILLIAN SMITH

# THE

# JOURNEY

*If I put out the light of my own personal experi-*
*ence I cannot see and I cannot judge the experience*
*of others.* —ERNST CASSIRER

THE WORLD PUBLISHING COMPANY
CLEVELAND AND NEW YORK

*Library of Congress Catalog Card Number:* 53-6643

FIRST EDITION

HC 154

---

## ✌ PROLOGUE ☞

---

THERE IS no going alone on a journey. Whether one explores strange lands or Main Street or one's own back yard, always invisible traveling companions are close by: the giants and pygmies of memory, of belief, pulling you this way and that, not letting you see the world life-size but insisting that you measure it by their own height and weight.

But you forget this. You start out feeling free. Your bags and your brain are packed full of supplies and facts for your trip, all the things you think you need. And then you get on your ship or plane or whatever, set for places you have not seen, friends you have not met—and suddenly something is there beside you, whispering, Better not look at that, better not listen; come, I know a place . . . a person. . . .

What a talent these companions have for luring us into dead ends! And yet, I could not have done without them. For though there were a few memories, an old worn-out belief or two that almost stopped me before my trip had begun, there were others that opened doors wide. And it was by their help that I found, at last, what I had gone in search of.

5

I went on this journey to find an image of the human being that I could feel proud of. I wanted to reassure myself of mortal strength, of man's power not only to survive on this earth but to continue growing in stature. I wanted the faith to believe that we can fulfill our role in this evolving universe of which we have been given such awesome glimpses.

*We human beings. . . .* What haunting words! A tune one knows and can never quite begin and never quite finish. Did they hold a real meaning for me? I was not sure.

The trouble was, I could not match the words with a clear image. Too often I could not see the human being at all, so hidden is he behind masks of political differences, of color, and spurious normalities. Long ago, I had torn those masks—they were cheap in my sight—but the person behind the mask? Had I caught more than a glimpse now and then?

It has not been easy for any of us, lately, to keep the image of man bright. Even in our own minds it has been trampled down, flattened by totalitarian beliefs that we are not aware we hold, torn by the Censors who fatten on our fears; made conforming, "normal," animal-like, machinelike, absolute.

Five words that have no place in human values. For men tied fast to the absolute, bled of their differences, drained of their dreams by authoritarian leeches until nothing but pulp is left, become a massive, sick Thing whose sheer weight is used ruthlessly by ambitious men. Here is the real enemy of the people: our own selves dehumanized into "the masses." And where is the David who can slay this giant?

I had been asking this for a long time, as have many others. One day, I realized that each of us has to find this David within himself. It is a job, like breathing, that no one else can do for us. And yet, I know too that as each discovers afresh the person within him—as sculptors and painters, dancers and writers, the poets and the prophets and the scientists put down in their unique ways what they find, the search grows easier for everyone. It is the individual's task, yes; but it is also this generation's historic mission to find and set up in a high place the human being revealed in his manifold differences and infinite possibilities, for all to see, to be exalted by, and to identify with.

And so, I went on a journey to answer for myself a few questions: What are our most human qualities? What sets us apart from animal and machine? from the masses and the monster? How can we believe in our infinite possibilities when our limitations are so conspicuous? And hope? What is this stubborn thing in man that keeps him forever picking the lock of time? that drives him to measure his puny size against the unknown —and win? The odds are against him, the odds have always been against him, and he knows it but he has never believed it. And because of his refusal to believe it, because of his crazy unconquerable hope, he alone of living creatures has learned to outwit fate and to enjoy the job so much that even on holidays from stern necessity he keeps challenging his antagonist. It is a strange talent, and strictly human.

I wanted to learn more about this mighty resource. And there were other words, old, encrusted with clichés: faith, and freedom, and risk, and that poor battered word "equality," and love, and life, and death. I needed to know what meaning they held for me.

What I sought, of course, was something to believe in; something that intelligence and heart can accept, something that can fuse past and future, and art and science, and God and one's self into a purposeful whole.

A few of my questions were never answered; others changed into new questions, for I changed as I went along. Slowly I began to understand what, perhaps, I had known a long time without understanding: That man's unique qualities and destiny begin in the unchangeable fact of his brokenness. He can never be whole though his integrity has come out of his reaching for wholeness. He is forever laying a plank across the chasm, relating himself to time, to people, to knowledge, to God, narrowing the gap between dream and reality, creating more and more ties— And yet, he still feels alone. On the milk of his loneliness is nourished everything he loves and delights in, even his future, but the ache remains.

The story I have written down here is concerned with not only what I learned but how I learned it.

I knew that what I sought was too humble, too proud and enduring and fragile to be found among generalities and abstractions. But I did not know where to look for it. I began my search by reading: poetry, philosophy, novels, scientific journals. I studied photographs of dancers, of faces, hands, for the spirit of man cannot be torn from the image he holds of his body. I went to museums, looked at sculpture, paintings, drawings. I talked with surgeons who know so intimately the brokenness of the body and the courage that binds a life together again. I read memoirs and letters. I was groping; feeling around; looking for maps that might take me where I wanted to go.

During that winter, I watched a young man whose body was paralyzed learn to move again. I had never before seen the creative spirit spelling itself out so plainly. Then it was that I learned, with a paraplegic, the passionate meaning of movement. I watched him the day they tied him to a board as if he were a mummy and stood him on end, on nerveless feet that were as full of emptiness as a wraith. He blacked out. But the next day, he stayed in this world and participated in his bright triumph. He was a man, standing up. Bound to a board but *here*. And slowly, I saw the change come. He learned to sit; to get in a wheel chair and slide out again. Inch by inch he was regaining his universe. Then came the morning when he stood on his feet, alone, clinging to the bars, but he stood.

I went away for a few months. When I came back, he was walking slowly down the parallel bars; sliding himself from end to end of that strict little path. Then, almost suddenly it seemed to me, he was on crutches, standing; not walking but standing as he learned to swing his crutches above his head, in front, behind, above his head: getting what they call "crutch balance." One day, he walked. I stood there watching him with the same deep feeling of miracle that I have each time I see Martha Graham dance. It was so beautiful a movement, rigorously disciplined, God knows, bound by an iron reality; but within the limits set by dead nerves he moved with grace, and with what I think of as an immense inner freedom.

As I watched this man I thought, Martha Graham could understand this triumph. For she, at the other end of the arc of human movement, has the same mastery of body and spirit that he now has. A paraplegic and a great dancer . . . each pushing back the frontiers of the body, and the mind, each with a free and bold imagination clearing the way for the human spirit to move to levels not yet attained.

Sometimes as I have sat in the audience watching Martha Graham dance, it has seemed to me as if she were unwrapping our body image which has been tied up so long with the barbed wires of fear and guilt and ignorance, and offering it back to us: a thing of honor. Freeing, at last, our concept of Self. Saying to us, The body is not a thing of danger, it is a fine instrument that can express not only today's feeling and act, but subtle, archaic experiences, memories which words are too young in human affairs to know the meaning of.

I went home, to the mountains. If I could understand not how nations meet ordeals, not how Man meets his, but how one man, one woman, one little boy, one girl met theirs, what defenses they drew upon for their hard moments, if I could see the human being in them, working, creating, surely I would find what I journeyed in search of, for only in ordeal is a man revealed at his most creative. Then it is that the hidden forces of a life show themselves working on the side of human growth or on the side of death.

I came upon bits of what I sought in the most unexpected places: there was an afternoon on 51st Street, at Toots Shor's; and another in an old lost graveyard on the coast of Georgia. And in a café, one night, a paratrooper who had come home from a prison camp in Germany helped me understand the largeness of life and the smallness of death. And there was Carl. And much of what I found came from my own memories, for I soon realized that no journey carries one far unless, as it extends into the world around us, it goes an equal distance into the world within.

And now, I sit here turning the pages of the manuscript. The book is almost completed.

As I read what I have set down, I see how personal a book it is. It is not my life's story, of course. It is only a handful of memories, a few experiences, mine and those of people I have known. I have used them as a sculptor uses dabs of clay, pressing them on, one by one, until finally an image is made of what a human being looks like to me. As I write, I am thinking of a morning when I was in the clay room at my camp watching the children work. There they were: each with a lump of clay, smoothing, pulling and turning, picking a little off, pressing a smidge on, until it changed slowly into an image of something they dimly saw and felt. So gravely they worked. One little girl said, "I am making something nobody in the world has ever seen." And when it was done, it was her own small face. She was right. No one had seen it before for it was herself as she felt herself, with her secrets spelled and misspelled in the clay.

And that is, of course, all I have done. I have put down here an image of the human being made from my own experience of life. Its meaning is the meaning these memories hold for me.

## 1

I HAD been reading a long time.

On this day I awoke early. I went down to my workroom, taking a cup of coffee with me. And sitting by the window which looks out on the mountain, I picked up a small book. It was written a hundred years ago by a British surgeon, Dr. W. J. Little. The first book in English on cerebral palsy though that name was not used then. No one knew what to call this trouble which twists into such cruel shapes the muscles and lives of little children. It was still a mystery and we do not like to give names to our mysteries.

I had happened upon the book by chance, and read a few chapters hardly knowing why I read them. Becoming more absorbed as I turned the pages. Laying the book down to wonder at this man who dared explore an unknown—and in those days, almost taboo—area of human misery. Because he was concerned about children, one day his mind was illuminated. He thought, *Something can be done for them*. That magic phrase! Why is it that a thousand of us, ten million, maybe, will not think it and then one day it is said aloud by someone and suddenly a life is changed, a town, a period of history.

I read on. I said to myself, *In our town there was*—and forgot to read more. I was remembering:

I was nine; he was ten. We stood at the corner gate of our lawn. I was crying. He had brought me a Christmas present. And I had just told him that my mother would never let me accept it. She had not let my big sister accept a watch from one of the high school seniors, saying it was much too expensive a gift to be suitable. If my sister in high school could not accept a little old watch, I knew my mother would never let me accept this magnificent five-pound box of chocolates wrapped in gold paper and tied with a pink satin bow. Between my sobs I tried to explain. He leaned on his crutch, holding the beautiful box, and cried too. And when I saw his tears I buried my face against his crutch and really let myself go.

It was then that he took command of the situation. Why not ask her, he suggested. I dared not. He put the package down on the sidewalk and while I wept he went to our house to ask my mother's permission to give me this gift. I thought him brave and beautiful as he swung back along the path, nodding his head to tell me the good news.

Martin never seemed "different" to me. Nor "crippled." There was a heavy brace on his leg and he used crutches; but it seems to me now that the brace and crutches were piled up in our minds with bicycles and skates as simply another means of moving around in our world. He lived in a big brick house and sometimes after school I went home with him. We ran first to the kitchen for a piece of cake—it was the only home I visited in where there was cake every day; afterward, we went to his playroom. But before I left we always stopped in the dim foyer downstairs to look at the sculpture that lined the wall. They were plaster casts, most of them: a marble or two, a bronze—reproductions of old Greek and Italian and French pieces. In the shadows of a corner was Venus of Melos. I thought her very beautiful. I did not think her a cripple because her arms were gone. She always seemed whole to me. I would stand there, dreaming . . . swept into a world where there are no words. Just as she was, I loved her—as I loved the little boy who took me in to see her.

And there was Midge. She did not live in our town but each summer she visited my playmate's family. Midge was small. I did not know her age but she was not as tall as I when I was eight years old. Each summer when she came, my little friend and I had grown an inch or two but Midge's height never changed. She was deaf too and talked on her fingers. We envied her this special ability to make words with fingers as much as if she had talked in French. I always thought Midge a wonderful person. She had so much to say. She had traveled with her parents to faraway places. She had seen a queen. I do not know whether her queen was "real" or one in a play or a circus. It does not matter. She had seen a queen and we admired her for what her eyes had embraced. Because she did not talk with her lips and tongue we learned to talk with our fingers. I never learned to talk with only one hand as she did but I was proud that I understood her lightning-quick language.

Of course I knew Midge was "different." She was different just as my brother who played the violin was different from my sister and me who only played the piano.

They were my friends, these two: people I knew and loved and admired.

There was also Carl. I did not love Carl. I was afraid of him.

I believe, when I was little, I was more afraid of him than of anyone else in the world. I did not know a bad thing that he had ever done and yet he seemed as capable of evil as the Devil. He could not talk. He made sounds without consonants and we laughed when we heard them. Sometimes we could not stop laughing. We would stand there and laugh and laugh and laugh and he would look at us and grin and slobber and try hard to say more to us. This was the signal to take to our heels. The moment we began to run, Carl ran after us. Laughing, falling down, he would chase us. I could feel him coming closer and closer and in terror mingled with deep and awful pleasure I strained to escape him. It was like bursting out of a nightmare to elude his big hands. And yet, when he fell down we stopped and waited for him to get up again. We would stand there, breathing hard, alert, watching him struggle to his feet—ready to streak out the moment he moved toward us. Down Main Street, across vacant lots, behind stores, sliding around garbage and boxes of trash, on through the alley, on by the town water tank, on to the calaboose—

I can still see it: a small roundish building, octagonal in shape with barred windows in each of its sides. The town's lockup for the casualties of Saturday night, the drunks, the winner in the razor fight, the loser in the craps game, and now and then another loser who was waiting to be transferred to what we called the "lunatic asylum." A very interesting place to children—and rarely did we fail to run by on our way from school to stare at the new faces and to talk to those who would talk to us. The game with Carl reached its enchanting climax here; for as we ran around and around the calaboose, faster and faster, the inmates would take sides and yell for us or for Carl and sound and movement would go whirling until the whole earth was reeling with us. Then suddenly it ended; we lost our breath or Carl fell down.

It was when he had chased us once down the alley back of Miller's Dry Goods Store that he stumbled and fell hard against the big wooden boxes piled there, cutting his face until blood oozed out in a thick smear. He lay still and we stood watching him. We were afraid he was never going to move again. Then he got up slowly, like a big broken puppet, and made a lot of strange sounds. This time I did not laugh. I wanted to go home, quick, and we left him alone there.

I could not sleep that night. Wherever I turned, there was Carl crawling to his feet, making those sounds. There was so much blood. I lay in the dark staring at him, then in a quick flash, somehow, I could not see him at all. It was as if he had gone around the corner. Where? Where would he go with the blood streaming? Who? Ah . . . that was when the hard little question lodged inside me. Who was there for him to go to? I had never thought of Carl belonging to anybody. He *was*. That was all. Just as was the Devil. Just as was the ghost which old Silla used to tell us about. Just as was the torn awning that flapped in the rain, making gurgly sounds as we ran under it into the post office for the evening mail.

I got up and went into my mother's room and felt her face with my hand until she opened her eyes. I told her that I had a bad stomach-ache, and she, knowing her child, let me curl up at the foot of her bed until morning.

I could not tell her that my mind ached, that a little green question had blocked its smooth peristalsis until all of me was twisted in colicky pain. I just lay there with my hand on her foot, touching her flesh, believing in her closeness, believing in an earth made solid because my mother's feet walked on it, until finally the little question slipped away and I recovered the old indifference, the old ability not to see which keeps grownups at ease and lets a child go to sleep.

Questions which cannot be freed by words find it easy to slip into the blood stream, changing the body's chemistry, changing a whole life, sometimes. I struggled to find the words that night with which to ask my mother about Carl but there were no words. It was a shocking thing that swept me beyond words: this stabbing possibility that Carl might belong to someone. If he belonged, he was real, like me. If he was real then there were a thousand more questions—and my mind was too young to carry the weight of them.

I did not try. I was used to a world where questions were not answered and usually not asked. The lights had not been turned on in childhood when I was young and sometimes it was a very dark place as we children groped our way, each finding his own path through the mysteries, laughing and crying in the wrong places, trembling at harmless things and sometimes accepting the brutal with ease. So I pushed Carl back with the rest of it: with birth and death and the Devil and God and my own body and other people's bodies and broken dolls and ghosts and colored people and sin and the long still look that sometimes I saw my mother give my father. And I forgot that day.

There was another time, so small a moment: I was older, in my teens, I think, for I seemed of importance to myself in a special way. Somehow I was at the town's water tank, listening to its drip drip drip. When I was little I liked to go there, I liked to stand under it, feeling the coolness, the wetness, the glistening green of the old fence nearby. And I went by again, as if to add a little coda to an almost finished childhood by repeating a few measures of the old games. And there was Carl standing there too: listening, feeling the coolness. I went over to the fence and touched the damp green growth and he pulled himself over and touched it, and then he bent and pulled and grunted—I can even now see the sweat on his face in that cool place—and wrenched a piece of the mossy stuff off and handed it to me, and I took it and whispered Thank you. I walked slowly away until I was around the corner, then began to run wildly as I used to do until I reached my home.

It was later, two or three years. I had gone one night to the drugstore with my brother and he had left me to look for a friend. I went outside and stood on the quiet street. The block of stores in front of me was faded out in the darkness of our little town which had no bright lights in it, though I could fill in the sequence of meat market, empty vegetable bin in front, barber shop, hardware store, the lawn mower Mr. Brown always left out and the big plow, the sacks of seed pulled just inside the door, and at the end of the street the poolroom with one small light reddening it. I walked down the side street by Salamander's Café listening to the laughter, the voices, but dared not stand there for it was for colored people, and knowing I was out of bounds I turned and started back to the drugstore. Then I met Carl. He was looking in a window of a darkened store. He pressed his face against the glass, then he moved on to the next window and peered inside its darkness; then on to the next, and the next until he reached the drugstore where I stood. He came near and said "Ar," and I said "Hello Carl." And we stood there looking at each other for a long time on that dark silent street and then I went quietly slowly home, not waiting for my brother.

I left my home town when I finished high school and did not see Carl again until the day he walked into a novel I was writing. Suddenly he was there on the page, just as he used to wait around the corner for us to come from school and jump out at us, making his strange sounds. And I saw at once that he was big and powerful. It was as if during the years when I had forgot him and the world had forgot him, Carl had been feeding on our unasked questions. Now he was a giant. And I knew this "village idiot" who belonged to nobody had somehow affected every life in our town— for there is nothing more powerful than ignorance, not even intelligence; and rejection is a bond that pulls men together like elastic until they smother each other.

## 2

My town that follows me wherever I go is not the town a tourist would see or the Chamber of Commerce would claim; nor is the Carl I remember today the real Carl. My memory of him would match the real person no more than the house whose rooms I am forever returning to in search of what a child left there, would match the piece of real estate to which my parents once held a deed.

The memory has so little talent for photography. It likes to paint pictures. Experience is not laid away in it like a snapshot to be withdrawn at will but is returned to us as a portrait painted in our own psychic colors, its form and pattern structured on that of our life.

It is a curious thing not that this is so but that we seem to forget it. Always we expect it to return unchanged. But always when we lay it away, a wonderful thing happens: a new experience is created out of its secret union with ourselves. It may be that we store away a small, a most trivial conversation and suddenly one day it stomps back to the surface of our mind big and brawling, having fed on the raw-meat emotions it found there. Or we lay away a walk we took once with some-

one we loved, our mother maybe, and one day it comes back a
flowery path where the seeds of our happiest dreams have
sprouted. Or, sometimes, we press back as far as we can a
moment that broke the heart, we think we have walled it away
forever, and then smeared with clown's paint, tippling cap
and bells, it slides by the watchers and comes back to make the
world laugh, and maybe to stop our own tears.

With facts, the memory behaves more sensibly. A fact can be
photographed and laid away to be returned to us, sometimes, in
quite good condition—if we keep it separate from our own
desires and feelings. Our childhood, never. And yet, it is no
less true because we cannot see the original again.

Because my memory of Carl is a portrait not only of him but
of me and my town and our ignorance and fears, I see him even
now sometimes as a giant. To reduce him to a life-size person
like Midge and Martin and my other playmates, to paint him
in the soft warm pleasures they wear in my memory is near to
impossible. I find it so hard, of course, because I never accepted
him as life-size. You don't accept a mystery: you peek at it,
run from it, you think about it at night, you dread it and dream
about it, you laugh big, and sometimes in your panic you hurt
it but you don't ask it over to your house to play with you. You
just push it back, deep down in the darkness where it sucks on
other mysteries, other feelings, other fears, growing bigger and
bigger until a day comes when you feel small and defenseless
and suddenly it is there, confronting you.

Midge was called "deaf and dumb" by people in our town.
That is not a pleasant phrase. And yet it did not spoil my
esteem for this gay bright girl whose fingers danced like a tiny
ballet corps, nor did it drive her into that region of the mind

where fear stays. She was not one of the mysteries. No one
suggested that she had been struck dumb by the Devil, or had
stopped growing because God was pressing her down with
His angry hand to punish a grownup in her family. Had they
whispered such paralyzing hints, I am afraid this little creature
might have changed not only in memory but right in front of
me into a lump of grotesquerie, like the Cocteau film in which
the Beast and Beauty's young lover dizzily change faces, or that
terrible moment in *Lost Horizon* when the camera turns the
young girl into a wrinkled leathery old hag before her lover's
eyes. Such metamorphoses are not limited to films and fairy
tales and children's dreams but happen in grown-up minds, too,
when pressures grow hard. Then it is that the inside of us
turns over and throws out all that is down there—the anxieties,
the unasked questions—searing, like an acid, those who are
nearest us, and most different.

This did not happen to Midge in reality or in my memory
of her because I knew a few facts about her and had accepted
her as one of us. We children knew she had had measles when
a baby, that this had caused her to lose her hearing, that she
did not speak because she could not hear words. The facts were
incomplete, for Midge could have learned to speak had only
someone taught her; and the facts did not explain her tiny
size, but at least they made sense. And Martin's crippling made
sense because we knew he once had a disease of the bone caused
by an infection. We understood that these two little friends had
suffered hardships and we respected them, I think, in that silent
way of children, for having come through their difficult experiences just as we respected the Swiss Family Robinson for having
survived their shipwreck.

But what we knew about Carl did not make sense. We knew only that because he staggered around and dropped things and could not talk, he was "crazy"; he could not go to school (or if he went he could only sit there), he was different, and there was no place for him, anywhere. And we knew from the whispers that he was like that because somebody in his family, maybe, had done something bad; and now he was that somebody's clumsy sin made visible, put here to shadow grown folks with an inescapable threat and to teach little boys and girls like us to be good.

Such a grisly story. . . . But no one knew a better one to tell us in those days. Our parents had never heard the words *cerebral palsy* or *spastic paralysis*, nor had I until long after I was grown, nor had our neighbors, nor most of the world. In our little town, we used words like "crazy" and "idiot" so easily. To us, they were synonyms. To us, they fitted many people who were different in looks or ways or beliefs. We did not try to enlarge our vocabulary because it matched so well the dimensions of our knowledge. If the deaf did not speak we called them "dumb"; people who could not talk though they could hear were "idiots." The idea that a child's mind might be full of words but his throat and tongue and lip muscles unable to say them because he had been injured before or during birth did not enter our heads. We did not know that there are motor centers in the brain which affect your leg or arm muscles and other centers which affect your power to understand the meaning of words, and still others, your ability to speak. Nor did we know that a lesion in one of these centers might make it impossible for you ever to pick up a glass of water though you might be the author of books or solve mathematical problems

with ease, nor that a part of your brain might not finish growing though the rest of it grew just as it should do.

We knew we would choke and die if lungs were without
oxygen too long but we did not know that the brain can be so
seriously injured when deprived of oxygen for a brief time
that one may forget years of one's life or, if a baby, may never
discover how to move at all. The Rh factor, the blood types,
were not yet in the dream-stage of young scientists' minds.
Blood was "blue" to us if two or three generations of a family
had lived in big houses; and the only other blood typing we
had heard of, I am afraid, was that done on Main Street by
looking at the color of a man's skin.

But even had our parents known these facts, they could not
have talked to us. They thought it so wrong to say aloud the
names of important things, to put into words their feelings
about the experiences that meant most to them. They could
not have told us that Carl's brain had been injured in birth or
just before birth, because they could not have brought themselves to mention his prenatal existence to children. Those nine
months a baby spends inside his mother were in those old days
as dishonorable a topic of conversation as if they had been spent
in jail or in a state asylum. A disesteem had fallen on man's
image of himself and on his most cherished and tender relationships, and because of it, silence slid over the peaks, into the
deep valleys of human experience.

Had we only known a fact or two . . . maybe we children
would have accepted him as one of us. And accepting, maybe
we could have helped him rig up a way to communicate with
us—just as we worked from morning to night in vacation

stringing up lines from tree to tree so that, perched high in our tree houses, we could still keep in touch with each other. But the mystery of him made it too hard.

It seemed so close, suddenly—that little town. I felt as if it were here reading the book with me. In those chapters were the answers to Carl—not all of them of course, but enough to tear the mystery and let the facts in.

This book was published in 1853. Seven years before my mother was born. . . . I am sure that she never heard of it, nor our doctor, nor most doctors of that day. The medical societies of England honored its author by calling this group of paralyses "Little's Disease," after his name. Once naming it they did no more about it. Seventy years passed, almost eighty, before anything was added to what Dr. Little had observed. Only now and then did a doctor use his knowledge. Seventy years is a long time for children to wait. Why did they have to?

I sat there, turning the question around in my mind. Of course there were many reasons. But one, I think, had to do with the ways in which we protect ourselves from evils that we cannot deal with. My parents, other parents, the doctors, the priests and preachers, and writers, and all who spread good and bad news across the earth, had built up defenses, as had the generations before them, against disasters that were too hard for them to bear. They had called Carl's brokenness "God's Will"; they said there was a "mysterious purpose" in such troubles. They, like all human beings, used words and faith to take them across chasms which scientific knowledge had not yet found means of bridging. And when words would not serve, or faith, then they erected high walls of silence and secrecy to keep themselves from seeing the chasms. How could they have lived otherwise!

This surgeon was "ahead of his times." His heart and imagination and intuition had boldly explored what other doctors had ignored, feeling it to be useless to try to help these children —feeling this way partly because organized knowledge had not yet "proved" what Dr. Little had "guessed," partly because adequate technics of dealing with the trouble had not been found, and partly because they, too, like ourselves had once been children, had heard the whispers and felt the chill mystery seep to their bones. And so, after honoring their co-worker, they turned away to the acute diseases of the body which they believed could be cured. And there were plenty of them that needed a cure in those days.

That is the human way. We build up our defenses slowly, brick by brick, cementing them with our fear and anguish; and then, when they are no longer needed, we cannot bear to tear them down. We have leaned on them too long. Our lives have been shaped to fit them, psychic muscles have stiffened against them, emotions have learned to flow under them, our vocabulary has entwined itself around them until they are almost hidden from us.

And so, the little Carls, the childish fears, grow into giant memories—invisible traveling companions that follow us into our grown-up lives. Then, when decisions must be made that may affect our happiness or our children's welfare, or maybe the whole world's future, these giants push the adult in us aside, sometimes, and put *their* mark, not our signature, on the page of history.

I had not planned to go where that hundred-year-old book had taken me. My maps led to other places. But the memory of Carl kept pulling me down old sandy paths. . . . And so, my journey curved here, going for a little way back into my life and the lives of people I had known when I was young.

# 3

It was Sunday afternoon. I was driving along the coastal roads of South Carolina and Georgia, trying to recover the feel of the country where my family once lived.

I had left the highway and was on the back roads. Roads that I did not know. I would see one and take it, hardly more than a sandy streak through the pines, and let it lead me back into the past if it could.

All day I had been going along slowly, fusing with the sun and swamp, the ragged swinging shadows, the ugliness, beauty, the old beat of things. A palmetto moving in the wind, the dry swish swish of it in the dark . . . the smell of a turpentine still . . . a wet patch near a ditch yellowed with pitcher plants . . . and suddenly one sees everything again, all of one's childhood, everything but one's self—*that* little ghost has just gone into the sand, the shadow, the bay tree.

Again and again I had come across lost avenues of twisted cedars through which the eyes travel so easily to a house that is rarely there. Sometimes the chimneys remain; now and then a garden of boxwood and briars; once through a formal avenue

of century-old trees I saw a bright-painted roadhouse spraddled
out like a prosperous whore sunning. And down the road, an
hour beyond, there stood a gray two-story house whose Vic-
torian gingerbread verandas were so like those I had run over
a thousand times as a child that I felt as if I had stumbled
across my home town.

The colored folks from the farms were going to church,
walking down the hot sand road, most of them, in dresses
bright as stick candy (the women and girls), in shoes not worn
all week and white hats (the men and boys); a few riding up
quick in a ramshackle car, shouting quick, slamming on brakes
quick, then slowly opening the car door, and getting out slow
and saying howdy, soft and slow, in sudden shyness.

They would stand around in front of the church set back
in the shade of pine or oak, maybe in broiling sun—not anxious
to go in yet, liking it there. Talking. Women shrill, men deep-
voiced. Bright sounds, too far away to form words for my ears.
Then they would laugh. Not only with mouth but with muscles
and tendons and nerves and glands and bones and skin and
memory until the whole body was rippling and washing and
changing its shape into a new thing, fresh and new, cleaned of
tensions, freed of resentment. Laughter that struck down the
Whiteness, struck down poverty, struck down sweat and shame,
laid it flat on the earth, made it nothing, made them big big big.
It had been a long time since I heard anyone laugh like that and
I was caught up in my past—so unchanged was this moment
from all I had known long ago. Here on the coast, tucked in
by creeks and marshes, moving slow as the tide were people
floating in a back eddy of time. They knew so little of what has
tightened the hearts and minds of the rest of the world; and yet

I had the feeling that maybe they knew more, deep down in them, where knowledge is a real thing.

After a time they would go in, I thought; they would take off their white hats and tiptoe in and sit there waiting on the rough benches, and somebody would go to the little reed organ if they were fancy enough to have one, the preacher would step up front and open his Bible. . . .

And after a time, they did. Then I drove up closer, sucked into the emptiness, and listened to the singing. They had left laughter outside and hate and shame with their whisky bottles and their six-day life and were singing to God of something that He and they understood. It came out of them as if from a bottomless pit. It flowed and settled in a pool of still-ness, it burst out like the thunder of water rolling over a precipice, and as suddenly was no more than a whisper. The men stopped singing. A woman was telling God now. I could see her through the window. Outside, before the service, she had stood apart from the others—a tall thin heavy-boned woman, the color of pitch pine, with big restless hands that looked like they had wrung out a thousand washes. She had on a pink straw hat, pinned back from her face, and her nose was high and thin, and she had that stern proud look I have seen on streets in Egypt and India. Now she was singing. She sang her feelings clean across to heaven, she sang her hope and her hurt and my hope and hurt, and yours, she made God bend down and listen to something that no one has ever put into words, for only in those fabulous sounds we call singing, that flow from a deeper level than words, can it be told.

And now, once more, the men were singing with her: soft at first, low; then it grew strong and loud and angry in its urgency. They were telling what it means to be human; singing of loneliness and separation, of darkness and light, of heaven.

It had come too close now, and I drove away out of the sound of it, letting my eyes drift with the marsh-grass toward the line of forest beyond, and back down the twisting creeks out to sea.

But you do not so easily drive away from memories. I kept thinking of my childhood; and of this woman as she stood there tall and straight and humbly proud, communicating with God. She might find it impossible during her entire life to talk once to a white person of what was in her heart and mind but she could tell it to God—and the white folks who heard would understand her meaning.

All my childhood I had listened to it: this never-ending dialogue between human beings and their God. Sometimes it took place in our kitchen: the woman whom we called "the cook" was hurt, there was pain that had to be expressed, anguish that needed to be understood, trouble whose limits must somehow be defined. Then would begin the singing. A voice without words would tell its story for the whole universe to hear. I have heard that wordless song, sung by women over washtubs, in kitchens, out under the oak trees when a white baby was being put to sleep. I have never heard a man sing it. His songs are different; they have words; or they are sounds that accompany body movements in work; but the women made of their voices a terrible and beautiful instrument which pierced the heart and the heavens.

I had heard it, too, in the little churches on the edge of town; only then, they sang with words for they were talking to each other as well as to their Creator. When I was a small child I would lie in bed at night listening to those sounds that pounded like the sea against an iron wall. Sometimes, lying there, I sang with them but more often I cried, not knowing why but feeling the loneliness of it, feeling too, maybe, the pressure of wrongs that could not be named in a child's vocabulary. And I knew, even then—it seems to me now that I knew—that they were talking over the white race's head to God, and in doing it, they made of the white man no more than an overseer; their Master was on their side.

Such people could never become real slaves; for in sharing his God with them, the white man made it impossible ever to keep them in serfdom. Maybe deep down in him he knew this, the human part of him, the God part, knew; and even as he snapped the lock, he handed his slave the key. It was only in those few bitter decades just before the Civil War that he tried to get the key back. Then it was, when "race" had become a three-edged thing, an economic and political and moral issue, that a part of the South made one last effort to justify itself by saying the black men had no souls. And during this time Bibles were taken from some of them and they were forbidden to come together in churches or in any place. But nobody in his heart believed it for a moment; neither white nor black believed that their relationship with God had been severed.

There is an old song which Virginia slaves used to sing at their funerals: *Come down, death, right easy.* You wonder as you listen, how they did it; how they found so naturally the simple right words for those tones that press down to the bottom of your soul and make it ache with all that is sad and bitter and tragic and triumphant not only in their life but your own.

Come down, death . . . right easy . . . they'd sing, as they lowered the body roped on its narrow board down into the hole. And someone would lift the palm of his hand in symbol of "God's Book" and make up words to say, but the words often faltered for it was hard to remember what was in a Bible you had never read. Then, those standing around that hole would begin to sing; they would sing the body into its grave, sing it on up the long road to heaven . . . sing it straight into the presence of God.

And so, because long ago a few white folks decided that their slaves had no souls and hence needed no Bible and no preacher to help them die, our South and the whole world were given the most poignantly beautiful death songs a folk ever created.

How strange and lovely, sometimes, are the wages of sin!

Now in these confused times there are those who try to cheapen this rare and honorable page of man's relationship with God by telling Negroes that to sing spirituals over radio and television "stereotypes them as slaves and primitives." It is true, these old songs have left a sign on all who have sung them; they are marked—*not* as slaves or primitives or clowns or animals or cogs in a machine but as the sons of God: men who have held on through terrible ordeals to their faith and dignity. And we, who listen, have a sign left on us. We are not the same afterward; for it is not granted one, often, to come as close as this to the grandeur of man when he refuses to live or to die except as a human being.

Song and laughter, and prayer . . . I kept thinking about them on that hot Sunday afternoon as I drove down nameless sand roads. As long as our laughter can turn giants into pygmies—whether those giants threaten us inside our minds or outside in the external world; as long as feelings can be communicated in song when words are forbidden or when feeling is too deep for words; as long as prayer—our last line of defense— is available to us, the door to the future of the human race cannot be irrevocably closed.

And yet, I had taken these magnificent defenses for granted until lately; until I began to realize that the freedom to laugh, to sing, to pray can be taken away from us, too, by power-hungry censors who try to dehumanize man. Censors who may be inside our own minds, for it is not always demagogues and dictators on the outside who strip us of the resources and relationships that are most precious to us.

I was remembering a young friend. She would see no reason for this journey. She was so eager for "action." To stop for a little while and think—when there is so much to be done! "How can prayer and song and laughter be of value to us, today? To Negroes—like me? How can they be? What can they do for us in times like these? They have certainly not torn down segregation. That is what we want down: the walls."

Yes, and I want those walls down, too. I would like to see every one of them down tomorrow for I know they have almost smothered the goodness in us. But after they are down and we stand face to face—will we recognize the human being in each other? We may not. For in the struggle for something we call "freedom" it is easy to lose sight of the reason for that freedom. We (white and colored, Jew and Gentile, Westerner and Asiatic) want the walls down so that the man in us can have

a chance to grow; but in our struggle we may give ourselves
a mortal injury if we do not take care.

In no way are we more likely to do it, I think, than by banning from theater and television and radio what is misnamed
"racial and religious stereotypes"—a phrase that is presently
used to define characters who do not flatter a group's image of
itself. What a curious upside-down conformity this banning
could bring about! For it is not stereotypes that are disapproved
of but a certain kind of stereotype. With sincere motives these
self-appointed censors insist that no play, no motion picture, no
novel show a member of the Negro race (however real the
character may be) in domestic service or working as a "menial,"
or one who attempts to maintain a harmonious relationship
with a white southerner, or one who is "happy" down in the
South, or laughing and singing and dancing. No Negro woman
may be shown in love with a white man though a white
woman may be shown in love with a Negro man. You may
write about a Negro intellectual however nasty in his snobbery
and however poorly realized as a character but you may not
show a blackfaced sweaty farmer in blue jeans struggling with
the complexities of human toil and relationships and in the
struggle finding an equilibrium, a serenity; no, if you do this
you have made of him an "Uncle Tom" and of his wife a
"handkerchief head." You may not put a Negro waiter, honest
and hard-working, in a movie but you may put there a Negro
businessman who made his money perhaps by exploiting his
own race, who is a stuffed shirt and dull and greedy—but if he
plays golf that is all right; for white folks too make their money
sometimes in questionable ways and are sometimes stuffed shirts

and dull and greedy, and play golf. It adds up, alas, to a parvenu
gaucherie—this racial "line," this new stereotype. But no matter! Tear off the old black mask; put on the new white mask.
What a sad and true thing that when we hate someone a great
deal we borrow from him the qualities that gave him power to
harm us, and wear them like a crown!

And the human being beneath the mask? the real person?
different from all other persons, struggling, aching and paining
and dreaming and laughing and loving his life sometimes no
matter how hard it is, building up the defenses he needs, trying to find fulfillment in whatever way he can, reaching out
for a relationship with himself, with other people, with his
earth and his God? where is he? He is the "invisible man"
made so not always by the white race but sometimes by the
Negro himself, and by his friends who want to "free him."

And it seems never to occur to these would-be censors that
what we need on stage and off stage, in books and in life, is
people who are real; who follow no "line" save that marked out
by their own life, and their hopes and dreams.

Stereotypes of course are distortions of the truth about men;
never are they made of pure lies. For they have to do with the
ways and means a hard-pressed man holds on to in order to
survive. Caught in a trap, what does he do? If he is sane he
develops defenses that will help him endure what he cannot
escape. The Negro group had powerful resources within their
bodies and memories and fantasy life and they used them; they
found more resources in the white man's religion and the white
man's ambivalence (which they reckoned with so shrewdly)
and they used these too. They developed these defenses to a
conspicuous degree which in gifted individuals resulted in

works of art enriching the whole world, and in others bent the
personality sometimes into grotesque and sometimes into utterly
beguiling shapes.

And yet, as this was taking place in those old bitter years,
something else was happening, too. Individuals among the
Negro group knew individuals of the white group who were
decent and they loved them; and these decent individuals returned that love. Ah . . . I know how humiliating it sometimes
was; but not always was it a shameful thing. There was understanding; there was a shared sorrow and a shared respect; a
guilt they both knew; they stood over many a coffin together—
sometimes the coffin contained a body they both loved, sometimes it held a man's cherished dream.

With this profound knowledge of each other, how then were
the stereotypes formed? by whom? By those who, refusing the
insight and wisdom of their own personal experience, tried to
justify a situation which could not be justified. By those who,
finding tragedy unendurable, tried to turn it into farce and
melodrama, or sometimes tried to forget it. When we want to
cheapen a man (or our relationship with him, or our memory
of him) we make with our words a cartoon of those defenses in
his personality which have served him well, or those which
have needled us most deeply. We distort them (by enlarging,
by omitting, or sometimes by mating them with our own secret
vices); we try to cut them down to a size that cannot hurt us;
we try to turn them into weapons which we can use against
him (or against our own guilt). So we stereotype. It is a powerful means of carrying on a cold war—whether that cold war is
with our own conscience or with external enemies. A man loses
in this cold war when he is willing to throw away his defenses

just because the enemy has caricatured them. He loses a second time, I think, when in his hate and confusion he tries to assume those qualities which have hurt him worst.

It is a familiar thing, this stereotyping and this identification. We see it so plainly in the warfare between parents and children; between men and women. A child becomes like the mother she fears and hates . . . so often making her own qualities that have harmed her most, discarding her identity (or perhaps never finding it). A woman wants her "rights"; she resents being stereotyped as a "female"—so what does she do? She gives up her feminine resources and tries to snatch from man his maleness, or his masculine privileges, and now and then his worst style of life.—And there are Americans today who have begun to look bloodkin to the communists whom they claim to abhor. . . . It is such a worn-out old story; why can't we human beings lay it away, bury it, and begin a new and more interesting one!

As I drove along that Sunday afternoon with the woman's singing still in my ears, I was thinking of these troubling matters. Remembering my young friend, brilliant and sensitive and lovable, who wants to "fight for her rights." "Oh, I don't want these rights given to me: I want to take them. Legally," she said and laughed, "not bowing and scraping, hat in hand, begging for something to be returned to me that is my birthright."

"Did your parents bow and scrape to white folks?" (In a lifetime spent in the South, I had so rarely seen servility in a Negro—always with the bow and the scrape there was a faint mockery; the tongue was in the cheek—and anybody who wasn't a fool knew it.)

"No. In my family we always talked back. Not in a loud voice, I've been told, but we talked back. My aunt says, we did it sometimes with our words and sometimes with our eyes and sometimes with all the bones of our body but we did it."

"I like to think that you did."

"Maybe they sound like a child, such words; but it is good for the spirit to protest. I believe that."

"I believe that, too," I told her. "And then a day comes as it did for the people of India when talking back is over. As segregation goes, and it is going fast now, we have something harder to learn to do."

"I know," she said quickly, "to forgive."

And that requires of us a deeper pride, something more real than arrogance; something both the white and colored races have to learn. Something beyond scorn and resentment—

"I wonder," I said aloud, "how many of us can find this humility—in time."

"I don't know. I know only that it is hard to forgive when you have been wronged so deeply."

"Almost as hard as it is to forgive those you have wronged."

She laughed and her eyes filled with tears. "I am all mixed up; you are; everybody in the world is, I guess. This sloughing off, layer after layer, until you find something real at the core is a terrible job. But I still say the praying and the spirituals have not got rid of segregation."

No, perhaps not. And yet the pounding of those sounds through the years against the conscience of the world—surely it weakened the barriers a little, surely a few holes were torn in the walls. But whether it did this or not, it kept the people behind the wall human through a terrible ordeal and that is an important thing. Now today, what substitutes have we for the prayer and the song?

Prayer. . . . I knew that I did not understand it. I recognized its great power but I did not understand how a human being relates himself on so deep a level with God. It might be a wordless relationship, as I felt in the singing of the women. It could be made with words. I am sure it is no easier to pray than it is to create music or write a poem; it must be as hard to do as it is to build a bridge, or to discover a great scientific principle, or to heal the sick, or to understand another human being. It is surely as important as these to man in his search for his role in the universal scheme of things. That role? I hoped to understand it better on this journey, somewhere.

To pray. . . . It is so necessary and so hard. Hard not because it requires intellect or knowledge or a big vocabulary or special technics but because it requires of us humility. And that comes, I think, from a profound sense of one's brokenness, and one's need. Not the need that causes us to cry, "Get me out of this trouble, quick!" but the need that one feels every day of one's life—even though one does not acknowledge it—to be related to something bigger than one's self, something more alive than one's self, something older and something not yet born, that will endure through time.

## 4

IT was on this day that I saw so many old family graveyards. I had counted six as I drove along that morning: small, most of them, and crowded by palmetto and swamp bays that had crept up close during the years. After I left the church, I stopped at one: a sandy little place, hot sunny no trees near, squared off by a beautiful iron fence patterned in fleur-de-lis. Inside the fence were eight baby graves covered with prickly pear and sandspurs. The inscriptions were stained and dark but you could read them: Here were Mary, and Jessie, and George Suddeth, and Clara Lee, Hoyt, and Thomas Purviance, Martha Lou, and Gracie Bell— all belonged to the Timberlakes and all had died before they were four years old.

- I wondered where their parents had gone afterward, for they were not buried here with the children. I thought of the thousands of stone lambs and carved lilies that strew a period when children died quickly and parents were helpless to stop it, remembering as I stood there that it was not a hundred years ago that this happened, not far away in a hot poverty-stricken backward region on the other side of the world but here at home around a bend of my own life.

I had almost forgot those old summers full of death, and the long illnesses that stretched into months sometimes, nibbling at the body until there was not enough strength left to hold life in it. The "fevers": scarlet, and typhoid, "continued," and yellow, and "chills and fever"; and the dysenteries and whooping cough and diphtheria, and all the rest of it.

Death came easily and often to a family for no one knew the cause or the cure of such devastating diseases. There were no hospitals except in cities, and so few nurses that one appearing in town, white and shiny in her starched uniform, was like the advent of the angel of death. She was there, and we knew it, to complete rites which the family were too exhausted after their long vigil to go through with. There were few serums and antitoxins; vaccines were used for smallpox but for no other diseases. We had not heard of X-rays; nor of blood plasma; nor dreamed of antibiotics. There were few laboratories even in the cities. Only a half dozen homes in our town in that first decade of the twentieth century had screens and inside plumbing. Why should they, for only the few had heard of insect-borne diseases or water that could be contaminated by drainage. As for bacteria and invisible "bugs," they were hearsay talk. In my childhood there was still an immense skepticism as to the possibility of such notions being true. We knew the human body was surrounded by invisible enemies, but who those enemies were we did not know. And there was as much foolish talk and absurd precautions taken as are taken today against that unknown enemy "communism." Our nurse hung asafetida bags around our necks whenever a case of scarlet fever appeared in town, or diphtheria. And though our mother smiled she did not stop it. Even she, deep-down, hoped it would work. And it did stifle our fear by diverting attention to the repugnant mess six inches from our nose.

Far away, there were scientists working . . . learning minute facts, slowly putting pieces of the puzzle together, stopping now and then to make a new machine, to perfect an instrument that might help them see more clearly, returning to add what they found to this image of the body that was slowly taking on dim but fascinating shape and significance. But most of us did not hear of their work for the body and its health and its diseases were not news in those days.

The winters were full of illness, too, but for the children the summers were the bad time. School would let out in late spring, April or May, and we would scamper home knowing that we could now go barefoot. We looked forward to the ease, the emptiness of days, our tree houses, our secret gardens, the play children make up by themselves. We were glad, but we felt a dread, too, like a splinter working through you, for we knew some of us would not be in the next grade when fall came. Not because we had not passed but because we had died of "the fevers" that were already by the time the bays bloomed, spreading over county and town and family, over everybody, sinking in to the bone, shaking you as if an animal had you in its teeth. You got well or you died. Children in war countries must feel as we did: it was Something That Happened. We did not sit around brooding, never talked about it, went on playing; but deep inside, in that silent place where a child's fears crouch, it breathed.

And because of this Thing That Happened, our vacation days were sprinkled with funerals.

We went to those funerals as all children in small towns used to do. And sometimes, when it was a little playmate who died, we sang the hymns at the service. I remember singing in that choir, feeling as if hickory nuts were lodged in my throat, pride driving the tears out of my eyes, driving them down into the veins of my memory. . . .

And afterward, we played death with our dolls: chanting *dust to dust*, singsonging *Man that is born of woman is of few days and full of trouble he cometh forth like a flower and is cut down he fleeth also as a shadow*—burying the little doll-corpses in candy boxes and perfume cases, smoothing the mounds of dirt, and covering them with flowers, sometimes putting as many flowers in our hair as we laid on the graves, so in love we were with our living selves. Then we would dig them up a few minutes afterward and blow the dust off, and bring them back to life. And after a little while, we would bury them again, repeating it, repeating it, until death began to shrink into a little man, a flimsy little old man who could not even hurt a doll. And then we would shout and laugh and turn cartwheels and climb trees and carve our initials at the tiptop of the highest branch so that our names would be close to the sky, and make toadfrog houses and go on picnics and forget, forget, forget.

As I stood there looking at that little rectangle with its eight small graves, I could smell again those gardenias. For funerals came when gardenias were in bloom and friends gathered the waxy white blossoms from bushes in their back yards and brought them in homemade wreaths (browning almost at once in the heat) to tell you they were sorry. Everyone was sorry. No one knew what to do.

A woman would tear herself to pieces on the prongs of shadows if she tried to fight a disaster as big as this. And there has been through the centuries a deep wisdom in human beings that forbade them to do so. I do not believe Mrs. Timberlake fought it. I think she accepted. She called the death of her eight babies "God's Will." She said that God's ways are inscrutable, that He is merciful and would not have brought this sorrow upon her had there not been a reason. And she believed her own words. Perhaps she said (I heard my mother's friends say it when I was young) that Jesus gathered them to Him to save them from a more fearsome trouble for there are things worse than death, these sheltered women would add sadly. Far worse, their friends would echo. Maybe He reached down, this Friend of children, and gathered them "like flowers" before the frost, before this inescapable Something touched them. What was this dread thing? No one ever explained. For such Gothic imaginations as theirs, a phrase or two like this was enough to loosen a hundred ghosts and set them wandering. There was no need to give name to terror. The children were saved from Something Evil, they were "safe in the arms of Jesus," as the old funeral hymn reassured them. That was enough to know. Mercy had intervened.

Superstition? Ignorance? It is easy to use these words. But at its core this faith was so good and creative, despite its wrapping of irrationality, that it saved many a woman's sanity. It sheltered the ambience of life as a hand cups a windy light; it made survival a struggle worth giving devotion to, for there is

purpose in life, no matter how brief its span on earth may be—
a purpose that is not broken by death but only detoured; there is
something ahead, beyond the chasm; there is heaven—you have
to believe that, their hearts said.

I stood there, that Sunday afternoon, thinking of the faith of
these mothers, of Mrs. Timberlake's faith, of sudden disaster
and the ways human beings have of meeting it. Thinking, too,
of the cynicism that slowly eats away the bones of "normal
times," and of the obscene doubts, the sudden revulsions from
life that have recently pulled entire nations down below human
stature causing them to surrender their future to the past, as if
they no longer wanted it.

Mrs. Timberlake's faith made it impossible for her to surrender. She by-passed despair by handing her children to God
for safekeeping until she could join them. Her earthly future
was a deep hole—how could it be otherwise after such a loss—
but there was something luminous, another future far away
but *there*. She was sure of it. All she had to do was to create
out of her belief a slender plank on which to walk across that
chasm. And having known women like her, I think she managed it. Her faith made her able, as women through uncounted
centuries have done, to cook a good meal for her husband, even
as her present was breaking in two, and be glad of his pleasure
in it; it turned her gardening, her crochet and embroidery into
creative seasons which flowered her talents; it made it possible
for her to bear child after child with hope, with confidence
even, that this time, this time, she could take it through the
hazards safely.

Call it innocence; even so, its power is not weakened. It
worked. In the way of all creative things, this faith fused Mrs.

Timberlake's life into a whole, tied her past and future together, gave her sorrow dignity and form.

A little wind blew a whiff of sand across Gracie Bell's grave, curled around the edge of it, slipped into the sandspurs, pulled the grass open, revealed a sea shell: milky white, pink-centered, grated by restless sand until it was rough and porous.

I unlatched the gate. A rusty hinge fell off as I opened it. I went inside. A stone headpiece on which two curled-up lambs had stared for fifty years at each other told me that Gracie Bell had died in 1901. She had lived six months. Her grave, and each of the others, was edged with sea shells. Somebody—Mrs. Timberlake? her husband?—somebody had brought the shells from the coast twenty miles away and arranged them in those neat rectangles in the sand. There were many kinds, as if the shell gatherer had gone out morning after morning, and alone there—maybe at dawn when sea is gray and smooth and sky gray and the wet beach glistening like glass—had carefully picked up shells while flecks of bubbly color blew over them and the waves shsshed and now and then a sandpiper cried.

Over George Suddeth's grave a design of starfish had been spread like a seaweedy blanket (there was something about George Suddeth that set him apart, I could feel that) and on each of the other graves one starfish was pressed into the sand near the headstone.

Who in the Timberlake family had done this, I do not know, but somehow grief had spoken. Out of the sea and faith was woven a cover for disaster. And that seemed a miracle to me: this power of the human being to heal a wound, to capture the love set wandering by the loss of the beloved and hold it close again, to bridge the future: all this, with a little made-up thing. It may be only a starfish grave cover, or it may be a poem, a painting, an act of sacrifice. No matter. Out of the same profound hunger it comes: the need to restore what has been destroyed, to make whole what is broken, to keep narrowing the separation between man and his universe.

## ⋖ 5 ⋗

### MIRACLE. . . .

I can use the word now, but when I was young, miracles frightened me. I could not bear to read about them in the Bible or listen when the minister talked of them in church. They seemed uncanny, supernatural, something beyond the known, outside my experience and my parents' and other people's experience. Outside of Order, of Law. I feared them as I feared all irrational or sudden things: ghosts, angels, explosions, accidents—somehow they were tangled up together in my mind. And instead of being pleased when I read of a miracle, a laying on of hands that caused a man to "rise up and walk," I could not endure it. It seemed—if true—a terrible caprice of an unknown power suddenly interfering with human ways. It was "unfair." (I was one of a large family of children and I resented it, I suppose, as I would have resented my parents giving medicine to one child to restore it to health and refusing medicine to the others.)

It did not occur to me that a miracle might be a sudden stumbling upon an unknown law, a law that had to do with man's relationship with his universe. Relationship? What was "scientific" about that! And everything had to be scientific for me when I was young. I felt, as did so many of my generation, that we were at last stepping out of a dark tangled swamp of medieval superstitions and beliefs where mankind had been lost so long, where many were still lost, into a sunny open plain where facts could be clearly seen. If we could know the facts! I could not have believed then that the bright facts we sought so eagerly can sometimes shut out the truth as completely as can the dark clouds of ignorance. That was a knowledge too hurting for my generation to accept.

We had had too much mystery in childhood, too many unanswered questions, too much of our life had been left in the dark. Now we wanted only to get quickly to that open place cleared by science and lighted up with statistics and "proofs" that no one could question, with "laws" that could not be broken for anyone (not even the favorite child), laws that worked as impersonally, as mechanically, for man as for a machine. That was our idea of "science." It was actually a new word for "security." And every generation, perhaps, has to find its new word, for the search for security's synonyms is an endless one.

In my search, I rejected the unknown past and unknown future (sometimes bargaining away my memories and dreams) and headed straight for that Never-Never Land, the known present. There I wanted to stay forever. I liked to think of it as a cleanly drawn rectangle whose lines my mind—and heart—could trace, stacked up with neat little piles of facts. It did not matter how small if it fenced out anxiety.

How hard my generation tried to live in that small place! How desperately we tried to give up every belief that could not be "proved" (though I could never quite do it). It meant giving up the deeper presence, faith; it meant giving up so much that our fathers had cherished. But we did not care—as long as we could make-like a fact is superior to a belief, as long as we could make-like the unknown is only a dark closet where there is a switch (if you are smart enough to find it) that will turn on the lights "science" has wired the whole universe with!

We were scared. And like all scared people, we were greedy: we had to know everything. And yet we shunned understanding. Perhaps because understanding is a relationship and requires that you give as much as you take and we had so little to give. We were the takers. The "realists." The materialists. The empty ones who stuffed themselves—and in their generous moments stuffed others—with things and money and facts and figures. Nobody valued wonder and awe; they were outworn things, like tenderness and love, left in the nursery with unanswered questions and broken dolls, and broken dreams.

Now, one by one, we are returning from that flight from the unknown. Humbled, some of us; not rejecting science but no longer demanding certainty as if it were a human right; beginning once more to put the puzzle together, hoping this time that we shall not leave out the human being and his relationships with himself and with God as we almost did before.

As I stood there, on a Sunday afternoon, in a graveyard, making up the lives of the Timberlakes out of a little sand and a few shells and eight slabs of stone with dates and names written on them, I realized, suddenly, that *miracle* was a word I could use again.

I was no longer afraid of it. It seemed such a human thing,

something that has to do with God, yes; but with us and our beliefs and the laws of the universe. It is a wind that changes, I whispered (as I stood there looking at those little graves), that blows from a new direction. Why it changes, why the event occurs we may not know for a century, ten centuries, maybe never; or we may know next year, or even now, perhaps, someone knows. It changes; an unknown law is touched and like an invisible harp sends forth a new sound. That is the miracle. That is God "moving in mysterious ways"—a phrase which had frightened me as a child. It is this. But it is more. For man himself is deeply involved. It is *his* relationship with the universe that changes; it is in *him* that the new fusion takes place; it is *his* belief, hope, body, mind, and the laws of the universe that swing around, break open, come back together and form a new whole. Then something impossible becomes possible: the boat moves, the paraplegic walks, the sick mind gets well, the plane flies, the poem is written, Helen Keller communicates with her world, the flecks of mold slipped into the blood stream cure the disease—and the woman, Mrs. Timberlake, turns away from her sorrow and walks steadily across the chasm on the faith which she has flung to the other side.

Ah . . . but maybe—I stared at that lonely little rectangle set between the swamp and the sea—maybe there was no miracle for Mrs. Timberlake. Maybe she lost her belief in God's Will. Maybe Gracie Bell's death put too much weight on it and her faith collapsed. Then she became suspicious. Then benign power changed right before her eyes into cruelty: God turned from father to persecutor. He no longer loved her (and she no longer loved Him). He was doing this to her to punish her—for what? for what? That terrible question: opening a thousand doors into the past and never one into the future!

Could she have asked it? It is possible. It is possible that her love broke down, and she began an endless journey into the past accompanied by those words: *What have I done to deserve this, why did it happen to me, why why*—until the whispers gnawed her mind to pieces and they took her from that verandaed home set back at the end of the avenue of cedar trees and locked her away and that is why she is not buried here and why the foundations of the old house softened and crumbled (for there was no future in it to firm it) until one day a breeze touched it and its roof slid to the ground, making no sound.

It is possible. Families turn to dust as do nations when they lose their faith in the future. It could have happened to her. But I did not believe it. I felt sure that her relationship to God was too tender, too dependent ever to have been broken. She had leaned on Him as she had leaned on her father until she had become a part of Him. She would be faithful just as she was faithful to her husband no matter how grievous the hurts inflicted. She had bordered the graves with shells, woven a little blanket of starfish, borne child after child—

(It was late. I turned to leave that graveyard encrusted with its iron fleurs-de-lis.) Surely her faith had endured—I wanted to believe it—and had given her the fortitude to keep moving through the days, to keep believing in the purpose of human existence, to hold her hand around the windy light—

(I pulled the gate to, and turned away.) *But it had not kept her children alive.* The eight small graves whispered it as if my thought had been overheard: *Look at us*, they whispered, *it didn't help us.*

A cold wind was coming in now with the tide, blowing the grasses away from the sea. Back of me, the marshes were melting in the light of a sun going down, each blade flowed into the molten whole, dazzling, beautiful as is the faith of our fathers, but like that faith it did not warm me. I turned away. I wanted to forget the little graveyard and all it had brought back from my childhood and adolescence: the memories, the terrors that had not yet "been taught to sing."

In the twilight I drove on toward Savannah, toward the old place beyond it, down at St. Marys where my mother's family once lived.


No, faith in God's Will was not enough. It had survival value for Mrs. Timberlake. It kept her sane, I hope, and able to tie her days together somehow. But it did not keep her children alive; it did not ask the new questions that led to the flies and mosquitoes and outdoor toilets that had caused their deaths; it did not fight typhoid and dysentery, and build laboratories and X-ray machines and train scientists and discover penicillin. Alone, it was a breeding place for disease and ignorance. Alone, it can only dream of heaven, it can create no future on earth for the children of men—and yet, without it, those children cannot live as human beings.

The first part of that sentence I knew by heart by the time I finished high school. The second part required of me many years to learn. But it was the first part that turned us, my generation, in our doubt, to depend solely on science (on the Euclidean geometry-Newtonian physics-nineteenth century kind of science which was all we knew then, for Relativity and

Quantum and the Unified Field theories were concepts as un-
heard of by us as was Einstein's humble acceptance of limits
to human knowledge). It was knowing that it did not help the
children—had not helped us—that caused us to reject this
"faith" which our fathers and their fathers before them, having
so little else, clung to insisting it would do alone.

We were, each, so wrong. For neither the faith that they
leaned on nor the doubt which drove us to overvalue science
can make a future fit for men. No more than ovum or sperm
alone creates the child. Faith and doubt both are needed—not
as antagonists but working side by side—to take us around the
unknown curve.

But doubt, like responsibility, is not a word praised by men.
We sing our hymns to faith and freedom and fight our wars
for them, not for their grubby partners. Who buckles on his
sword today to defend responsibility! The few, of course; there
are always the few, or else there would be no new age. And
the few are important. "To be a man is, precisely, to be responsible"; Antoine de Saint Exupéry lived his words—on the
physical level by carrying out dangerous and urgent missions
for his country from which few volunteers ever returned. He
lived it, too, on the spiritual level as he slogged his way through
the clouds, crossed lonely deserts, for he was always searching
for and jotting down in his notebook not only data on the
enemy but his beliefs about man, about the meaning of tenderness, the significance of sacrifice, searching for a way of fusing
faith and knowledge and skill and responsibility and dreams
into a poetry of action and belief that can give wholeness to
life. "Each man must look to himself to teach him the meaning

of life," he wrote these words on a flight when death had been close to his plane all day, "it is not something discovered; it is something moulded," he finished his sentence.

*Doubt* is a word even harder to talk about, especially in times of change, for then its two faces whirl so dizzily. Look at it one way, it is so evil: the villain who cuts the taproot of faith, who spreads suspicion on the future, who jerks the curtain back at a man's weakest moment, who sends a heartbroken woman on an unlighted journey from which she may not return. Look at it the other way, and you find the stubborn seekers of knowledge, the imagination that can ask a new question, the seed of freedom, you find the man who accepts disaster not as fate but as challenge, and always you find the eternal pioneer in us who transplants faith, when necessity requires it, to a new frontier where it, in turn, makes a warm familiar home for the heart to live in.

So it goes. I wonder why it is so hard for us to accept these two partners out of which comes life, this dualism out of which unity is created. There is always a question, and an answer, before knowledge is found. We know everything creative that concerns human existence comes in pairs: freedom and responsibility, faith and doubt, the question and the answer, risk and security, the child and his grown-up self, past and future, wonder and certainty, pain and pleasure, male and female, sex and love, the dream and reality, victory and defeat, man and God. Keep them together, we have a whole, we have life; cut them apart, we find death at the center. Maybe this is the meaning of sin, I thought: for human beings to cut these deep relationships in two.

## ❦ 6 ❧

THE ROAD twisted low through
the edge of the swamp, crossed a branch. The highway was
not too distant; now and then, a roar of cargo vans floated
across from it but I was so deep in the past that it seemed to
come from a century beyond me. The sand was heavy and the
car moved slow. A cabin. A clump of sweet-smelling bay trees;
a dead cypress—bare broken limbs against the sky. A long
stretch of palmetto, a field, two cabins. Someone came to the
door holding a lighted pine knot and a hound rushed out close
to the car and slunk back as if he smelled the color of a strange
new age. Someone called *You come here, you,* and a little velvet
voice answered *Ya-hm.* And there it was close to me, a bit of a
thing, standing at the edge of the road. I leaned out and said
hello and it skedaddled quick to the safety of steps and there
was a ripple of laughter, and I said howdy to the rippling
darkness and the rippling darkness answered back howdy.

This was their country. It was mine too. And my mother's
and father's country. And all day as I traveled through it I had
felt as if I were home again going through old trunks, old
albums, old history books. My mother's family were rice plant-

57

ers; her father was a learned man; and always when I thought
of them, I saw the family as if in a mural encircled by a tide-
river and by my grandfather's books and big sacks of rice and
a bay with sailboats on it, and salt marshes, and old tabby ruins
and islands off the low sandy coast; and in the center of it all,
was my mother when she was four years old, standing at the
door of the attic listening to the whisper of rice spilling, spilling, spilling . . . for the Federal troops had steamed up the river
and shelled the nearby town and a cannon ball had ripped
through their roof and fallen in the attic and was embedded in
the sacks of rice stored there and for days afterward, as her
child-memory recorded it, the golden grains spilled and whispered and spilled and whispered until the attic was waist-deep
in the golden flood, and her mind was deep in soft smothery
disaster—and this is all she remembers of that war that tore
across the South like a hurricane, or maybe, more like a pesti-
lence or a bad dream.

My father's family were not of the tide-river and rice plantation country. Little Grandma belonged in my memory to
swamps and to lonely stretches of forest and wire grass. And
now it was swamp country that I drove through. The marshes
and the smell of brackish water and the tide-rivers were gone.
Only a few miles away, actually; but in the night, as in a dream,
places draw close together and become one—or suddenly
seem as distant as the moon. And as I drove down this lonely
sand road, close to the cypress swamp, past old clumps of bays,
I was thinking of my father and Little Grandma.

Her people were not planters but pioneers, Presbyterian
Scotch, who had come down from North Carolina into the
lower part of Georgia when the eighteenth century turned into

the nineteenth. It was frontier country full of sunshine and longleaf pine and cottonmouths and Seminole Indians. The white man and his government were driving out the Indians, pushing them into that Spanish territory called Florida, killing off those who would not go. All had not yet been driven out when Little Grandma's family moved there, and her childhood was full of raids, bloody victories—and quiet sunny days of danger when a shadow glides up, slips a knife in a back, and glides off into the swamp.

Her father was Captain Dave, who took part in this cruel business of driving the Indians from their land. Once he brought home two little Indian maidens whom he had captured after their parents were killed by his soldiers. The wild things bit him and scratched at his eyes and slipped between his legs and tripped him up but somehow he held on to them. He called his wife—and his daughter, Nancy, and their two black slaves—to come see what he had brought home. There they were, the three of them: a tough old soldier, scratched and bleeding and sweating and grinning and two burning-eyed brown squirming growling little females. Nothing to do now, he said cheerfully, but to tame them.

It was like taming a pair of swamp cats. The little Indians ran around and around the rooms, climbing up on the bureau, on the chest of drawers; in the kitchen they shinned up the walls and clung to the rafters and glowered there for a whole day; they broke two mirrors (which frightened my great-grandmother and the Africans), they emptied dishwater into the pots of cooking food. And finally Captain Dave—who got along well with that shrewd Indian leader, Chief Billy Bow Legs, and was famed among the white settlers for his skill and daring in this guerrilla warfare—went into a panic and locked up these two little fighters in a small outhouse. The old warrior handed them food through a high window which he barred up as if he had a dozen catamounts behind it. The two little Indians screamed all day, all night. When dawn came, they hushed their screams and a low moaning began. It went on and on, low, interminable. Through the day, through the night, the next morning, those moans seeped into the house, filled the rooms, filled minds and hearts and conscience—until shocked at what they had done, were doing, Captain Dave and his wife could bear it no longer and let them loose, and the two little girls ran as if the whole white world were at their heels, into the twilight into the swamp into the blankness your mind puts up when it cannot bear to look further.

Captain Dave and his wife and Nancy, my grandma, never saw them again. But as I drove along that night I could almost see them, these little ghosts who haunt our family history.

When Little Grandma grew older she married into a slave-owning family—not the fabulous and rare kind you read about in the romances of the Old South but a Scotch-Irish Methodist farm family who had twenty or thirty slaves and lived much as prosperous farmers live all over the world: hard-working, hard-eating, and hard-drinking, a few of them. Men for the most part who loved politics and brush-arbor camp meetings with plenty of preaching and plenty of praying; who had a good stock of gamy stories and a good stock of fine meat in the smokehouse; who went fishing on warm cloudy days, and bird shooting on cool sunny days, and fox hunting now and then; who built big comfortable homes for their wives and brought them dress-lengths of fine silks, and silver and china when they went to the cities, but rarely brought home a book or a painting or a new idea. They were not far-visioned men, not aware of a changing world, not future-makers, nor too tied to the past either, perhaps; just a bit dull, maybe, in the heart and the imagination; capable of appreciating things and food more than ideas or beauty or the nuances of human relations. Strong men, energetic, with a streak of cruelty and a streak of kindness in their nature, frank to admit that slaving is wrong, never defending it (my family) but making the most of it, a pretty penny off it, while it lasted. People who were the salt of the earth in peacetime; who measured up bravely in wartime but who somehow in times of swift change, when a way of life breaks off and a new way must begin, rarely contributed much toward the bridging of the gap between the old and the new.

When the Civil War ended, the homeplace broke into fragments. There was, after all, no firm foundation beneath that way of life. Nancy's husband came home but never quite left the bitterness and the ruins. Not that he talked about it but he seemed still there in it as if the past had caught him and the right and wrong of it had wrapped its two-edged hurt around him. Or maybe it was the right and wrong of all of life that bound him so tightly. Whatever it was, Nancy's husband was out of the present, drinking his way out most of the time, talking it out now and then in sudden angry reminiscence, or shooting it out among the birds in the forest.

So Little Grandma, the ninety pounds of her there were, took over. She taught her nine boys how to plow, she plowed too, to show them; they planted the fields together, they hoed and tended; and their mother was always there helping, making it seem like fun, while the two small daughters played dolls near by and the baby lay asleep under a tree near the branch.

One day, as it slept in the shade on the cool bank of the branch, Little Grandma heard a snapping of twigs and saw, coming down the edge of the water, a swamp cat. A "painter." He was almost as close as she; not quite, but he could spring swiftly and she knew it. She did not take her eyes off him as she started slowly toward the baby. Each time she took a step, he did, each time she stopped, he stopped. She knew he had seen her. Whether it is true or not, the old pioneers believed that they could hold wild things with their eyes. His eyes looked straight into hers, and she dared not move as she tried to stay him by this hypnotic device. She called quietly, quickly, to one of her boys to go fetch the gun. She listened to her son's feet padding across the field to the house while she stared at the big panther, while he stared back, while the baby slept quietly on its shawl in the shade near the edge of the water.

It must have seemed a long time until she heard footsteps behind her and her boy breathing hard. She reached her hand back without taking her eyes from the cat, and her son slipped the gun in it. She checked with her fingers to make sure that the hammer had been pulled back—and then she took aim, pulled the trigger, shooting over her baby into the head of the animal beyond it. The cat dropped on the edge of the branch, the baby slept on. The big boy took the gun from his mother and rushed up close now and put another load in the cat, and then the other children pounced on it, dragged it out, shouting, laughing, rolling over and over the dead animal, imitating a panther's scream, walking with bent knees around and around it, swaying from side to side, as they screamed and laughed, making fun of its strength, going wild now. But after a little, Grandma put them back at their work and picked up the baby and went in to cook dinner.

I have heard it all of my life, this story. Little Grandma would tell it to us in her room in our big old rambling house in north Florida. She would sit by her hearth, wrapped up in her crocheted shawl, stirring her fire now and then, and tell us. And while she told it, we would be roasting pecans in the ashes, or sweet potatoes—because we knew that potatoes had been cooked that way, when she was young, and we wanted to try things the way she had done them. She would tell it and always it was a legend of reassurance, a story of human strength able to deal with what comes to a person day by day. Things are like that, she made us feel—this little lady who was more than eighty years old and still so slight and so strong. The swamp panther is always killed before it reaches the baby. She made us sure of it. How did you do it, Grandma? we'd ask for the hundredth time. Her blue eyes would light up, she would laugh and say, You take aim straight at the head, and you pull the trigger, easy.

It satisfied us. Then she'd say in exactly the same tone, Better look to your nuts, and we'd scrabble for them in the ashes and draw them out and cool them and they were brown-smelling and fragrant to eat. Or we'd turn over the roasting potatoes and she would tell us other stories about those days when dangers seemed to be outside of people and never inside their own minds. And always there was in her room—this room which we called "Little Grandma's" for years after she was gone—a feeling that nothing could win over life, not even death. Nothing could get into the room with her unless it shrank down littler than Little Grandma.

There were other panther and swamp stories and some of these our mother told us. One was of a long journey which Little Grandma made with two of her babies in a light cart drawn by her mare. The last five miles were through a stretch of swamp country: cypress, vines, water. Dark was coming on. And one of the babies began to cry. It was then that Little Grandma heard the scream of the panther. He is in the swamp, she thought, not close; and she drove along quietly. He screamed again. This time he seemed to be in the road back of her. She knew now that he had heard the baby's cry and was following.

(As my mother told it, the simple story line ran along in hushed tones but the scream of the panther she imitated in curving cadences, giving a steady crescendo to the story until it reached its peak and this is what we children waited for and shuddered at when we heard it. Partly because we could not bear the sound, could not bear the idea of our mother reaching back into animal life and touching with her own voice its brutality; and partly because in this role of storyteller she was unlike her calm, sure, cheerful, everyday self. It was as if she had put on a primitive mask, something that had to do with an unlighted life that we were not supposed to know about— or maybe she had taken off the calm, serene everyday mask. . . . Whether a mask had been removed or one put on we were not sure—and sometimes, I think now, that it was this uncertainty which left us so deeply shaken.)

The panther was following the cart, there was no doubt about it. Each scream brought him nearer. And now the mare snorted, trembled, stopped dead in her tracks. And Little Grandma had to persuade her to go on, had to talk to her standing there in the dusk, in that loneliness, while she held her two children close to her. Then, as suddenly, the mare broke into a canter and went swiftly along but the scream was nearer. Each time it was nearer. Down the road . . . a half mile . . . a quarter mile . . . a few hundred yards. . . . Beyond the branch there was a small settlement, a clearing; once there, the swamp cat would not come near. Little Grandma knew this; and soon they would be there, and suddenly they were.

A simple story, almost anticlimactic, but it frightened us to our roots. Perhaps it slipped a master key into doors we thought shut and locked forever. But it did more: it disturbed something close to the surface of our rational minds. The outcome of the story depended upon such chancy things: how near you happened to be to the clearing, how near the swamp cat was, how fast the horse cantered—or suppose the horse had not let herself be persuaded by Grandma's voice to get going. These unknown factors, so strongly modeled by our mother, shriveled Grandma's strength and ours. We, and Grandma, were puny things left to the mercy of Chance and the animal kingdom. We did not like it; yet we begged to hear it again and again— perhaps for the same reason as that of my six-year-old nephew who, one day, sat through a motion picture three times believing, hoping, that the little fellow his age in the runaway scene would, next time, not be thrown from his pony and killed.

After Mother had told this story, we would hurry to Little

Grandma's room for reassurance. "But weren't you scared, Grandma?" we'd ask.

"Of going through a swamp? Law, there's swamp everywhere," she'd say serenely.

"But the panther screaming—and coming nearer and nearer —didn't it scare you?"

"Law, law, there're always panthers."

"But Grandma, suppose your horse hadn't moved—suppose you had been a long way from the Crossing—"

"Better look now at your sweet potato. Pull it out here, in the ashes."

And then to recover our belief in mortal strength, we would ask for the story of the baby by the branch and the panther who was shot in the head just by taking aim and pulling the trigger easy. And once more, as we listened, we felt it come back to us, our feeling that we were almost as strong and sure about life as our Little Grandma.

Strange how a child holds a lasting impression of a person whom she knew for only a few years. There was so little out of which to form the solid image that I have of her: only a few memories that light up now and then, on a tiny stage, far away. But in those scenes, Little Grandma shines across the shadowy years, a symbol of reassurance and comfort and serenity.

And sometimes we grandchildren needed her. For though our mother never lost touch with human dignity and pride, as did that next generation of us who actually became ashamed of the suckling and eliminative and loving and playful processes by which the young of our species are kept alive and human, she had absorbed from church, from history, from whispers, from woman talk and from man talk, and perhaps from her own young mysterious impulses, a dread of this reservoir of energy called "the body"; as much dread, I suspect, as the savages had of fire, or some of us today have of the power within the atom. Like them, like us, her mind was too full of its potentials for hurt, to see, to be warmed by, to be exalted by its magnificent resources for the creative and the good. And feeling this way, she laid upon her children some of this dread, doing it in the most effective way that a dread can be transmitted to a child: with love and kindness.

And at these moments when we shrank in sudden fear from life, even from ourselves, Little Grandma called us into her room, drew us close around her hearth, and somehow healed our bruises—not by tearing us away from our mother; no, this was different from two influences pulling a child in opposing directions. For these two women were too harmonious as mother and daughter-in-law ever to be in conflict—though with feelings so different. It was rather that Grandma was a kind of first-aid station, or a Red Cross nurse, who took up where the battle ended, accepting us and our little sobbing sins, gathering the whole of us into her lap, restoring us to health and confidence by her amazing faith in life and in a mortal's strength to meet it.

It was a faith that I think she never put into words. For it was deeper than words. An organic faith, one might call it. It seemed to flow in her blood stream, to balance her endocrine glands, to keep the marrow healthy in her bones. It moved the traffic along her central nervous system; it made her aim sure. She never pulled a trigger hard in her life.

Born to live. . . . It was as if her body fitted in with the earth and its ways spontaneously; as if, in those secret places of the soma which scientists are now exploring, a rhythm had been set up with the first heartbeat, with the first expansion of the lungs, the first warm taste of milk; as if a balance had been achieved of those mysterious male-female hormones that are in all of us, of other hormones that have so much to do with our organic gravitation system, of all the elements, salts, minerals, that swim around in our blood and bones and brain feeding us and reminding us that we are earthly creatures.

And because the whole of her body was in equilibrium, she accepted it as naturally as she accepted today's rain, tomorrow's sun. It was a useful thing, too; coördinated; giving more pleasure than pain, holding within it the power to do what needed to be done, rarely failing her in an emergency. She must have thought well of something that had proved so trustworthy.

Grandma liked this little earth we live on—at least the fragment of it that she knew. I never heard her talk of heaven. Perhaps because she did not envy the angels, though I am sure that she held no prejudice against them. She probably loved to hear about them on a Sunday, sitting in church, moving her black silk fan slowly back and forth; enjoyed them much as she enjoyed her flowers or a winter sunset; but I don't think she yearned to be one. The human body was good enough for Grandma and this earth, her home, satisfied her.

This acceptance of life, never put into words by her but streaming through her voice and body and eyes and acts, extended to birth and death. Birth was to her a natural process; death was as natural. She accepted both. She brought twelve

children into the world and she lost ten of them in her lifetime. Of these deaths, that of her beautiful and cherished
daughter, Victoria, was the hardest to accept, for Victy died
with a terrible quickness of miliary tuberculosis. They called it
galloping consumption in those days and it was a mysterious
and dread thing. But Little Grandma accepted that too. Here
was something, a disease, that she could do nothing about; nor
could anyone, at that time, do anything about it. There are
limits to human strength and wisdom, and she accepted this
limitation. Death, to her, was not a special act of God's Will,
something inflicted for a "purpose"; it was an inseparable part
of the process of life. It was of God, of nature, of the earth, of
man. For a human being to die was as right in Grandma's eyes
as to be born, though I don't think she ever talked about it.

Even this grandchild of hers, who was deeply troubled about
birth and therefore about death, who kept believing there was
a way, if you could but find it, to read those first and last chapters of one's own story which the grown people said could
never be read, felt this profound acceptance in her and was
comforted by it.

As I drove along in the darkness, memories of her floated
through my mind. I knew that she would have said, Law law
law child, and clucked her tongue had she known that I stayed
so long on a Sunday afternoon in a little wind-swept graveyard
thinking about death and life and belief and mystery and
science and the past and the future and God—trying to weave
of these words something my mind and heart could accept.
Little Grandma could never have taken part in such goings on.

My mother would have understood better. She knew that fabulous place we call childhood, and remembering it had given her a hunger: for beliefs put into words, for insight put into words, just for words sometimes. For my mother felt almost as if in themselves, words have the magic power to take you wherever you want to go; that they can open up ancient paths and let you go through them, easily; that they might take you to heaven—a place my mother thought about most wistfully. But Little Grandma would not have used words. She would have given you, first, a roasted pecan or a sip of her nice warm toddy and then put you to work quick at something earthy, had she caught you dreaming or thinking. She would have pulled you from the clutch of old memories as if out of quicksand, would have slammed the door on imagination as if on the Indians and made you know yourself in relation to the earth on which she stood: tying you fast, if she could, to your five senses as one ties a windy tent to stakes, making you touch and smell and taste life, and hear it and look at it; making you move with it until your body became a part of its deep rhythm, as was her own.

She could not conceive of a hunger of the spirit. Hunger? That meant to her a need for a sweet potato, a piece of hot buttered corn bread, a cup of coffee, a pleasant joke with her children, a good night in bed with her husband. But the *spirit* hungering? What for, child? What do you want that "ordinary people" do not want!

I suppose one might simply say that Grandma could not see around corners and believed no "normal" person would try to. And those mortals who are always peering into the past to recover what was left there, always staring into the future hoping to make it take the shape of their dreams, in Grandma's eyes had something wrong with them. What you have once left, Grandma said, should stay left. What you thought as a child, felt, wanted, your relationships of that period, are over and done with. She could not have believed there might be a little unfinished business there. She could not have accepted the knowledge that there can live in a grown person's mind a desperate child who keeps asking unanswered questions, who keeps hurting where broken relationships have never healed, who persists in wanting something that the whole world says you cannot have. If it is so, then certainly no one should talk about it, or even think about it. "Law law law," Grandma would have said. "Here, fetch me my gun, and we'll go out and kill us a panther or two; but keep that door inside you bolted tight, you hear!"

This lack of imagination, this refusal to budge from the solid earth and her five senses and the present moment, to explore either past or future, served her well as a pioneer woman. It kept her aim sure; it helped her pull that trigger easy when face to face with swamp panthers and cottonmouths. Grandma's defenses were almost perfect for the external dangers that this frontier country was full of.

But when danger was inside a person, when words were needed to tie you to someone, or to your future, or to hold a relationship firm or to illumine it or recreate it, when insight into dim places in the human mind was needed, then Grandma turned away and closed the door. For her, this inner life did not exist—except one little room, maybe, with a hearth and a low fire burning where her ego sat quietly resting when not at work on the external world.

She had so much that we need today in this pioneer age we are entering: confidence, nerve, and poise and laughter and zest for life, and the power to organize body and brain quickly to meet an external emergency. And yet I knew as I thought of her that night, that she had met only half her challenge. She was a frontier woman of the finest breed in a country full of dangers but on the frontier of the human spirit her aim was unsure.

I had learned this slowly from my father, her favorite son. With him she had understanding. He was strong. And Grandma admired strength. He had affection in his nature, and hope and laughter, fun, sympathy—and these were feelings that ran through her veins. She may have been aware, a bit wistfully, that her son held a visa given him by his insight and imagination that permitted him to travel to places and times where she could not go, that he had a world view she could not see; but she understood his energy and ability to turn a dream into something you could see and touch—and usually into money you could use. Whatever his life was within him, he spent enough time in the outside world to leave his mark on it and it was a mark to make a woman proud, she thought, as was her father's, Captain Dave.

But there was her husband ... and her youngest son ... and another, another, and even another who could not live in this world in which she felt so at home. They were always somewhere else, never in the present, never here, but in a secret time and place searching for something they had lost or maybe had never found. And because they had no words to tell her what they sought and she had no words to ask, nor insight to see, they acted it out in ways that the world would not accept. Nor would Grandma.

Had these children been lost in the Big Swamp she would have taken her lantern and gone out to look for them. No external danger could have been threatening enough to deter her. But that big swamp of childhood . . . in which most of us get lost, at least for a little while? No. She could not enter it even to rescue her sons. She could not even admit that it existed for she had no weapon that could defend her against its "dangers" except the simple and powerful one of denying its existence.

She who was successful in coping with war and poverty and death and wild animals could not bind her children's inner world to the world outside them because she could not communicate with them either through tenderness or words, nor they with her, about the urgent and important matters which she had convinced herself did not exist.

But I am glad that I did not know this until I was grown. For no woman, surely, has ever been more serenely successful with so many grandchildren than was she. I can still see her . . . in her room, wrapped up in her big shawl, stirring a little fire and telling us her stories: always reducing trouble to a size that even the littlest and weakest of us could deal with.

So the second chance of mothering was given her. And this time, when her arduous tasks had eased and some of her conflicts had passed away, when her old age circled close to her childhood once more and she saw its dangers as small as they actually are, then she made of her role of grandmothering something so warm and reassuring that no grandchild who experienced it could ever forget.

## ⊷ 7 ⊶

WHAT WAS Grandma afraid of?

She did not know. Nor do I. I doubt that the wisest students of human nature could tell us. They would say only that Grandma was "afraid of anxiety." When Franklin Roosevelt electrified the world with his eloquent phrase: *We have nothing to fear but fear itself,* everyone who heard him knew he spoke the truth. We knew from the wisdom which the human race has accumulated through a quarter of a million years, that men can survive ordeal if they can survive their fears; and they can master their fears if they can master their anxiety.

What anxiety is, no one ever quite says. It is so without shape and sometimes seems to be almost without content. In olden days, men created ghosts—so urgent was the need to give form to the formless. Today, *we* create ghosts—so urgent is our need to give form to the formless. And our children? born and bred on scientific facts? "Tell us a ghost story"—or maybe "tell us about spacemen" they beg and we know they want to hear it just as we wanted to hear it, and our parents before us wanted to hear it: so that anxiety may for a little while be clothed in words and wander through the imagination as

74

respectable and accommodating spirits or "menaces" who will go away when the story ends.

But though we can never quite put the feeling into words, anxiety is not made of mysterious stuff. It is as much of the essence of earthy human experience as is tenderness. Both are feelings that begin to grow during the infant's prolonged helplessness; both are nourished on those inseparable needs of a child to be taken care of and to be related to a human world. Then it is, when we are so long at the mercy of the Mothering Ones, that we learn our private definitions of tenderness, and loneliness; of sympathy, and terror; of intimacy, and isolation. And then it is that we begin to cling to these secret meanings.

As I drove along that night, creeping through fog pockets, speeding up when the road cleared, the old loneliness came back. Even in a large fun-loving family, as was my own, it comes to the young. Without words, it comes. And suddenly, sharply, one is aware of being separated from every person on one's earth and every object, and from the beginning of things and from the future and even a little, from one's self. A moment before, one was happily playing; the world was round and friendly. Now at one's feet there are chasms that had been invisible until this moment. And one knows, and never remembers how it was learned, that there will always be chasms, and across the chasms will always be those one loves.

There are, there must be, children who do not experience this sense of separation so keenly. Perhaps their needs of food and oxygen and warmth and cleanliness were met so adequately, and they were given so much tenderness when it is meaningful to the young, and there was so little anxiety in the faces and hands of the Important Ones around them that they never learned of human loneliness. Nor, perhaps, will they ever realize how dependent they are, actually, upon the good will of the world for their survival and their self-fulfillment. (And in my heart, I am not sure whether to praise or pity them.)

But I knew of loneliness: and there were times when the feeling did not go away quickly but turned into panic too urgent, too intense to be contained in any word but *terror*; as if there were no bridges, and none could ever be built, and even were there bridges I could not trust them with my weight. When such anxiety comes, the whole organism crumples as if one's inner bridges have fallen, too. No learning takes place that day for the Good Teacher is not in the school room; the Inquisitor is there. And who learned a lesson that he remembered from an inquisitor?

But there were other times: wide stretches of serenity, smooth as sands at low tide when nothing more catastrophic than the print of a sea bird's claw or the soft turn of a watery shell breaks the smoothness. Days when I felt fused with my world, when the bridges were safe, when the chasms were so narrow that a mere plank would do on which to cross them. I had so much faith then: because I felt the tenderness of the older ones around me; I had said something and it was understood; I had told a daydream and there was sympathy given it; or confessed a fear, a hope, and others said they felt it, too; or told a joke and they laughed; or was hurt and something was done to heal the wound. So softly, at these moments, the ties are woven around us and All the Others, and our world. And feeling close to my fellow-beings and to the earth, I gave sympathy to other living creatures as naturally as a child breathes.

And there were the times—different from the days of oneness

with my world, different from the solitary moments of panic and terror—when I felt a small anxiety, but not too much. Just enough: for me to know I needed to change my ways a little, I must change or good ties would be broken, relationships would snap, bridges would fall, people would be hurt, I would be hurt; when I knew I must use my head and get the facts; must learn something I had never known before; do something I had never done; risk a little, a question, a few words, the breaking of a small tie, maybe, in order to hold firm a more important one. Time had come to tear down the narrow rickety bridge and build a new one strong enough to take human storms and two-way traffic. Time had come, maybe, to journey back into one's past and make life-size the memories one had left there; to look straight—if one only could!—at the consequences of one's acts.

These were the learning days: when tenderness and anxiety were mixed in good measures, and I gained whatever insight and foresight I now have. If we only knew how to mix them just right for each child. So easy it is at one time and so incredibly difficult at another—and one wonders why this should be. But like all the arts, this turning of a little human animal into a human being requires imagination and sympathy and intuition and a bending of the spirit and knowledge, yes. But more: there is need to risk the unknown, a little. And that is so hard to do.

Tenderness and anxiety. . . . How firmly childhood is cupped in two words. Let us admit that we cannot do without either of them. Without the anxiety which comes first out of child-helplessness, we would not so desperately need tenderness; without tenderness we could not have found the miraculous talents, the powers, which have changed us into human beings; and once finding them, we would not have developed them further had we not been urged on by necessity and ordeal to dream and bring forth the dream.

Words and symbols, art and reason, and memory, and concern and sympathy for others, and hope: I said them over and over again, that night, as I drove slowly down those sand roads of the past. Out of them has come the image of men we see and cherish when we speak of ourselves as human beings. Out of them, all we prize in our heritage.

*In the beginning was the Word:* It is a beautiful first line for the biography of the human being. We could not bear to change it. But it is not quite true. Before words, came a feeling between mother and child: a need to bind together again two mortals who were separated by the act of birth and who still required much of each other in order to complete a process of growth that is different from anything an animal experiences. Out of this need to be bound together and at the same time to be free, to be served and to serve, to give and to take, to support and to lean, must have come the miracle of words.

I would like to tell you how a group of children in my camp discovered this. Almost casually, they had begun to play a game which they made up about Earth Man. The old council fire, familiar to anyone who has been to camp, had grown trite and dull. They wanted to do something different. One evening, as we sat around the campfire, a few questions were asked about the growth of man as a human being. What makes us different from the animals? Is it fire? words? the wheel? the shape of our hands? What brought the change about?

The game began. The children played like they were Early Man who had not quite evolved into a human being. Much of the play was on a childish boisterous level of animals and Man threatening each other in the dark. It was not difficult for them to get into the mood for such play as we sat on the hill against a backdrop of forest and mountains, sky, and the near-darkness. After a time, so our game went, Early Man discovered fire. When his terror of it had diminished, he realized that not only did it drive his enemies away, it made him more comfortable. Once this was known, it became a highly prized possession and full of magic qualities. The children felt this and spontaneously made up a dance to express the magic; and another dance to express the anxiety which Earth Man had known before fire was discovered when darkness, full of noises, surrounded him. But even with fire, man was not yet quite a human being for though fire changed his world a great deal, it changed him only a little.

"Maybe it was his hands," they suggested. "When he found that his thumb and fingers could be used as a tool and he began to make things?" They decided that this was important but not quite right. "Because, once making things, everybody would forget unless the things had a name and they could talk about them." No, words must have been more important to Man, even than his hands.

There followed long discussions as to how Man had begun to talk. Some thought he evolved a sign language by which he expressed anger, fear, excitement; or told about a place to get food; or called a mate. This satisfied the group for a time and they played it out, in this way. Then one evening an older camper said, "But you could keep on like this maybe for a million years and never never talk. Animals make signs, too, but they never have a language."

"Why?"

"They don't understand about symbols."

"I don't understand about symbols, either," a little girl said.

"Yes, you do," she was reminded. "You play dolls and you're playing like you're an elephant right now. And that's what a symbol is: something that takes the place of something you don't have, or can't be. Something that isn't here but you wish it were here," the older girl said.

"Or maybe," said another bluntly, "a symbol takes the place of something you don't want here. Like a bear," she added, "or a snake. You'd rather make up a word for snake than pick one up, wouldn't you?"

"How did we learn all this?"

With the bright intuition which children show when encouraged to talk about human growth, they guessed that the human child learned about symbols because it had been helpless and dependent upon others for a long long time, and during that period had experienced both the security of being close to its mother and the anxiety of separation. "And when we felt separated," one said, "her voice brought us to her again. Maybe her words took the place of her hands, sometimes; or when we could not see her, we could hear and felt she was near."

"I wonder," said one small camper, "who made the first doll. She must have been a very nice mother."

"I don't think she made it," another said. "I mean, I think a father made it, or an uncle. He didn't have babies, you see, so he made something like one. Maybe he sat down one day and chipped it out of a rock, or something. And it was so nice and small that he gave it to a child to play with. Then all the children wanted them—"

"Words may have begun," said one, "when Early Mother sang to her baby." They thought it probable that out of those reassuring tones came slowly the more precise communication that words give. And this is the way, in their game, they played out the beginning of symbolic speech. To these children, it was the need to feel tied to the Absent Ones, and the hunger to belong to one's world, that started the human child on its way to words. "Real words," they said. For the sign language continued to grow, too. But it was words, symbolic speech, that kept those human ties firm and ever spreading.

It was a game they never tired of playing. An endless one: as Man met The Stranger, and at first killed him, and then so slowly over thousands of years learned to exchange gifts with him instead; as Man made his first tools, tamed the wild animals, invented the wheel and so on.

Such simple, naive play it was, yet rooted profoundly in the shadowy region of man's past.

Now as I write of those children, I am thinking of Helen Keller. Not long ago, I read again the amazing letters in which "Teacher" (Anne Sullivan) tells how she groped her way to that lonely little human being "imprisoned in stone." By using the only means of communication left the child—her sense of touch—Teacher patiently, gently, found her way to Helen's heart. Once there, she cleared an incredibly devious route to her mind and connected it with the world we live in when finally, one day, as the word *water* was spelled into her hand and she felt, at the same moment, the cold gushing water from the pump, the child began to realize that "every object has a name." For Helen, human speech had begun; and with it, a life that had in it love and concern for others and play and work and hope and wonder, and God. But it would never have begun, I think, had not the child felt the tenderness of this understanding woman from whom she received the gift of words.

There are millions of human beings with their senses intact who are still imprisoned in the stony silence of childhood where nothing "has a name" because they were not given large enough gifts of words and love when they were young. A part of them is free to grow, to communicate with the world about the world's concerns, but the feeling part of them, the human-relating part, is caught in silence and cannot be freed until, somehow, words and tenderness become fused in their lives. Then, maybe, they too will suddenly discover, as did eight-year-old Helen, that "everything has a name," even the experiences of their first years on earth. And knowing this, a light may come on in their childhood and they may see that the monstrous things they have feared since they were young are actually as weak and small as they were when, long ago, they became afraid. Then, perhaps childhood will become for them a green growing place where human experience begins—not a surreal desert where only ghosts and Things That Have Ended roam.

But my little grandma did not believe that childhood is a safe place for children to explore. Too long *her* childhood, everybody's childhood, had been full of unnamed dangers more terrifying than the Big Okefenokee held. There were a few Indians who could guide one through the Okefenokee. There were no guides to take her across the trembling earth inside her, she thought, and no paths that words could make from it to the outside world. The only thing to do was to stay out. *Stay out and don't talk about it!*

So she locked the door and went outside with her gun where dangers are "real." Real enough to be shot between the eyes if you take aim and pull the trigger easy; "sensible" enough to laugh off and work off. She never realized when she locked the door on her childhood that she had shut her children up in it and only the strongest of them would ever be able to find their way out again.

An old old story. . . . Grandma's silence served her well but it could not help the children. It was simply the best defense this hard-pressed woman could find in the prescientific, arduous, impoverished time in which she lived.

Perhaps there is nothing in all the world more difficult to accept about ourselves than the fact that the defenses we use to protect us from our fears will not always help those we love; but sometimes, will destroy them, and us. And few things more painful to do, even when we understand this most human fact, than to change them although new and more effective defenses may be at hand, and easy to use.

It is hard because we did not rationally choose them in the first place, and even now sometimes could not name them to ourselves. We picked them up before we knew their names, when we were two, three, four years old, and later, wherever we could find them: in our home, on the street, at church, in the back yard, or the alley maybe. We had to have something and we snatched what we could. Tenderness and understanding? Yes, if they happened to be in the home. Words? Yes, if we heard meaningful ones. Silence and iron curtains? Easily, if that seemed the thing to do. Faith in God's Will? Always, if we felt it to be a real thing in someone we loved. Facts? And respect for knowledge? Of course, if we were given them. Whatever was there that our individual organism could take hold of, we used.

And once finding defenses that worked, we held on to them, building with them our small security system against the threats of the universe. They may be good, made of stuff that increases in power and flexibility as the years pass; or they may be as inept as toy pistols and as dangerous as matches. No matter. To each of us, our system is the best. Even when the enemy is winning the war in our grown-up lives, we still are deeply loyal to it, for now it has become for us that precious thing: a symbol of whatever strength and quality our lives have had. The little system has turned into The Way of Life. It is, for us, the Tao—and not to be questioned.

And because we love it and cherish it and believe in it as passionately as only the child in us can do (and yet perhaps are secretly doubting it, too, in that part of us where reason stays) we turn and fight, sometimes with real malevolence, the private security systems of others if they come in conflict with our own.

So it goes. Each, finding incredible or intolerable the other's defenses; each, taking a tighter grip on his own; each, so sure *his* little security system is the only one in the world that will work.

And who is right?

There is, and most of us know it in our hearts, a valid test of a human defense: Is it also a human resource? Will it help us and at the same time keep our children growing? Are we sure that the doors to our future and our past are still ajar after we have used it?

Or is it something that will improve our condition now but make further progress for us difficult, and perhaps impossible? Does it win the battles and always lose the war? Whether our defenses are "right" will surely depend on the answers to these questions.

But how hard it is, when we are struggling with fears, to think beyond ourselves and the present moment. Even the most responsible of us is not in a learning mood on those days, days which sometimes stretch into years, years when the quiet voice of reason is drowned out by the cries of the terrorized child within us. Time is meaningless then. How can we master it enough to swing our intelligence up and down the decades, the centuries, scanning them to see what marks our acts are leaving on them?

It is, of course, an impossible thing for an individual to do in times of acute anxiety. There may or may not be someone who cares enough to help him, to point the way, to ask the question that will set him back on the open road. If there is no one, the dead end is reached. The little security system that the child put together long ago just wouldn't work for his grown-up ordeals.

But fortunately for the future of the human race, not all of us are panicked by the same event or terrorized by the same voice. There are always some who can keep heart and head steady enough to hold the door open even when the mob rushes it; some who know and refuse to let the rest forget that improvement and progress can lead in opposite directions, and often do; that progress is not real, however much improvement takes place, unless it keeps men connected with that great reservoir in which human beings have stored the records of their wisdom and errors, discoveries and art, and triumphs and defeats, and dreams of God; unless it opens up more and more possibilities for growth and for the enrichment of us as persons.

 8

I HAD come a long way down those old roads of the past. And now, suddenly, I was back on the paved highway. Neon lights blazed in front of me, advertising a motor court with tiled showers and Hollywood beds and carpeted floors and air conditioning, and television (for fifty cents extra).

I turned into the cindered area, parked my car, paid for a room. As I unpacked, I thought how Grandma would have mirated at these goings on. She had worked too hard all her life to get back for her children what had been "lost in the war" not to appreciate things and bodily comfort. She might have shaken her head over the innerspring mattress—it could never for her have taken the place of a feather bed—but the rest of it would have seemed to Grandma a fabulous advance since her day.

The manager of the motor court came to my door to offer a television set. He was of the swamp country, I saw now, as he stood there. He had the look that is left on a face when hookworm and malaria and malnutrition have done their destructive work early in life. And in his speech were the old accents which were natural to the wire grass and swamp people who found schooling as hard to come by in the old days as shelter and food. People who, in my childhood, were almost as remote from books and learning and science and art and comforts as are the peasants of China and India.

Now he operated a motor court, looked at television, drove a Buick, took a trip in a plane each fall (so he told me) to the World Series, and read a newspaper.

As I made use of the conveniences with which our scientific age has filled this motor court, set close to the swamp—old and mysterious and deep-rooted in time as our human past— I kept thinking of this man. "Everything in the place is mod-run," he proudly told me, as he flung open the door to show me the mauve-colored lavatory and the mauve-colored toilet and mauve-colored toilet paper. And as I stared at the splendor I knew that his sanitary facilities as a child had been limited to a wash pan, a lean-to privy and the ancient corncob. No wonder he was proud of participating in these modern times—

But was he?

Did he know where these things had come from? Did he have an inkling of the intelligence, the persistence and patience and rigorous honesty of the scientific method? Did he realize that the things, the objects, the inventions in which he took such pride, were only the by-products of courage and integrity and men's refusal to give up the right to question the old, to seek more knowledge even though their bodies might be burned? Did he know that this is a search that can never end so long as the human species survives? that when it stops, man will stop with it?

Of course not. He knew no more about the origin of all these

fine "modrun" things than he knew when he was a child
where babies come from. To him, modern plumbing, air conditioning, television, automobiles, refrigerators, airplanes, antibiotics and all the rest of it rained down from heaven. Or maybe
were here, as the rocks are here, and the good earth, and the
rivers, and the forests. Somebody just stumbled across them, one
day. Or maybe the stork did bring them— Anyway, however
they got here, he knows they are *things money can buy*. That
money cannot create them any more than it can make the
earth and the forests and the sea and the rivers, or a human
being, would seem to him incredible. As incredible as it would
seem to a Communist peasant in China, today, were he told
that The Party cannot create all these fine things for *him*.

How did I know? Was I reading this naïveté into him because he had been poor and ignorant in childhood? No. I was
guessing it because he had said to me, as I bought a newspaper
and signed my name on his guest card, "Old Joe's done it agin!
He's making em throw out the books now. And going to clean
out the schools and the colleges and all the Communist professors and them scientists. Tell you what I think," he leaned
toward me and dropped his voice, "I think every Communist
and Catholic ought to be run out of the country, and there's
nobody but Joe McCarthy who's got the guts to do it. And
while he's doing it, he can take the Jews too," he added and
laughed.

I signed my name on the card, put my car license number
down and my town.

Yes, I thought, as I washed my hands in that mauve lavatory,
this man (had he lived in that time and place) might have

helped burn Bruno at the stake for defending Galileo's right to look through a telescope and tell what he saw in the heavens. He might have enjoyed attending the trial of Copernicus. He would surely have hunted New England witches with as much relish as he gives to his fox hunting. Though he hates "the Communists" because they take away men's freedom, he, too, would like to liquidate all the people who differ from him. Ban them; ban the books; ban knowledge; ban the scientists, the poets, and artists and all the dreamers.

And he could not tell why he feels this way. He'd likely say, "because they are Communists"; or "because they take orders from the Pope," or "they're Jews and—" Anyway, they are dangerous because they "change things." And change is bad, he feels, although his way of life has changed more since he was a child than a dozen generations of men's lives had changed before him. And he likes the change: likes his car, his motor court, his refrigerator, and air conditioning, radio, television, paved road, and county hospital, and the fact that his children are not sick with malaria and hookworm as he used to be. He is proud that his grandchildren can go to college only he wants "Joe" to get there first and take out everything not safe for them to know and question. What is it that he thinks is not "safe" for human beings to know?

There was a knock on the door.

When I opened it, he was standing there with a pitcher in his hand—this "villain" I was conjuring up out of a few careless sentences he had spoken.

"My wife thought you might be thirsty. It's mighty hot and the café down the road is closed so she sent you some ice lemonade and a sandwich. There is no charge," he added.

It was extraordinarily kind, of course, and I thanked him warmly. Shamed, now, by my thoughts.

He hesitated, seemed embarrassed. Said, "Every Sunday night she sends over a little something for the last traveler who comes our way. She calls it her Good Samaritan deed. She's mighty religious—but she has her own notions, like all you women, I reckon." He laughed.

She had not been in good health, lately, he told me. Seemed to worry so much. Was mighty proud of their motor court but making money troubled her. "And we're doing pretty good," his voice was modest. "But," he told me, "Susie don't like it. All her life, her daddy welcomed the stranger and never charged a cent to nobody for spending the night. They was somebody to welcome, she was always saying, not to take money from. And how do you know you might not be sheltering an angel unawares?" He laughed. "If Susie saw the whisky bottles I take out of these rooms before she goes to clean, she'd not worry much about the angels."

"But no matter what you say," he said, "she hunts it up in the Bible and proves you're wrong. She's a great one on the Bible. Knows it inside out."

"Does she read other books too?"

"Nothing but the Bible, but *that* all the time—cept when she's cleaning up the rooms here, or cooking over at the house. Susie's a great one for keeping things spick and span. When she can't find no more dust, she sets down and reads. She knows Revelations by heart," pride creeping into his voice now.

"Will you tell her, for me, that I have never seen cleaner rooms? The court is very nice. One of the best I've been in."

"I'd call it the best, I reckon—being's it's mine and I worked hard to git it." He smiled and when he did, the tightness left his face. He turned to go.

I suddenly liked him. He had come a long hard way from that little cabin near the swamp to this fine place on the highway. And to get here had taken courage and resourcefulness and dreams and work and steadfast purpose. Qualities we Americans are proud of.

I must write his wife a note, I thought, and stepped outside to ask him her name. We stood under an old live oak, talking. Beyond it were other great oaks, beyond them a long stretch of palmetto and piney woods, and all the night sounds I had known as a child, and a sky like no other I have seen in my travels across the earth for it still has on it the marks of my youngest wonder.

"It's home to me," I said suddenly. "All this."

"Thought you come out of the mountains."

"I live there now. But this is home."

"Born round here?"

"Farther down." I told him: Across the Florida line. Close to the Suwannee River. "My father was from Ware County; Mother's people lived on the Satilla River, near St. Marys." The old ritual of Americans meeting each other.

"You don't say. I reckon I know some of your folks, maybe. My folks've lived right here for ninety-two years. Down the road a piece."

"Always, it comes back," I said, "when I drive down here. Things we used to do as kids" . . . picking violets on the banks of the railroad track . . . walking the trestle and racing the freight train to the other side . . . building toadfrog houses . . .

gathering pecans after it had rained all night—the ground would be covered . . . sweet potato pie . . . cane grindings. "I still remember how sugar cane tastes when the frost has bitten it. . . ."

Neither of us spoke for a long time. Stood there, remembering childhoods curiously alike, however different the houses our families had lived in.

"Yes," he said quietly, "it sure comes back, sometimes."

"There was a big magnolia I used to climb. I don't suppose a magnolia in all the world could be as big as it has grown in my memory since I left there."

"Might be. There's big ones. Biggest I know is one in back of our house, over there. My wife'd be mighty proud to show it to you in the morning. Folks come miles to see it. It's more than a hundred years old."

"I'd like to see it. We'd string the red shiny seeds from the cones, I remember, and wear them as necklaces."

"Had a little sister who used to do it. Sit all day stringing her a necklace and bracelets for both arms. Ma couldn't never git em off her. Would go to bed with them pretties on. She died when she was goin on eleven. The fever."

"I remember it: typhoid, and malaria—"

"It nearbout ruined Ma. She'd already lost five. Nothing uncommon in those days not to raise your chudren. But Sybie was the last and gittin along fine and it went hard with Ma, losing her. It's mighty different today. And do you know? The young folks don't appreciate it. My son's wife has four kids, healthy as pigs. Never a one been sick. But she's all time complaining about nobody to baby-set fur her."

A wind had picked up. Palmettos were rattling as bony

fingers played across them calling the spirits out of the graveyards—Who told me that? Frashy. It must have been Frashy.
I hadn't remembered it since childhood, until now.

"Well, better be moseyin back."

"Tell your wife how much I appreciate her kindness."

"Sure will."

He turned to go. A car slowed down, seemed to be turning
in. A Packard. Negroes. Voice with a Harvard accent saying, "I
tell you it's no use. Where you think you are—Paris?" More
that we could not hear. Then laughter. A raw, bruised sound.
The car backed, sped down the road.

In deference to the fact that a woman was present, he did
not say the words. He simply looked at the car, kept looking
until its taillight disappeared. Kept looking. Then he said, soft
and slow, "Somebody sure better run them Communists out
of this country quick. If they don't—see what will happen?
And lot more! They tell me the Kremlin's got em everywheres
—in our schools and churches, everywheres. Only thing to do is
take every book and go through it word for word and clean it
out. Clean em all out!"

"There're quite a few books. Might take a long time."

"O. K. Then burn em. Burn em all up."

"Well," as I made no reply, "better be gittin on to the house,
I reckon."

He walked away. Stopped. Voice friendly now. Easy. "Susie'll
be pleased to show you the tree."

"I may leave very early."

"It won't be too early for Susie. She's not much for sleeping.
Sets up the whole night, sometimes, watching the stars. She
claims the signs are almost right now."

"For?"

"The end of time. Just a little longer." He tried to smile. "You're welcome to come by, early as you like."

I thanked him and went in to room number eight.

The sandwich was very good: a slice of her Sunday-dinner baked hen with a whiff of the sage dressing clinging to it had been placed in a split square of fluffy corn bread. And she had wrapped up a piece of marble cake and sent it along for dessert. Moist and a bit heavy with eggs, in the old-fashioned way, and beautifully marbleized in its browns and yellows. The "ice lemonade" had slices of lemon floating in it and looked and tasted like all the lemonade I had drunk as a child at Sunday School picnics, only then it was in great wooden barrels.

I ate the Good Samaritan food. Gathered up the crumbs in the newspaper to keep Susie's floor tidy, dropped it in the wastebasket. Stood there, staring at it. *Then burn em up burn em up—*

All of this night—sights, sounds and smells and tastes and textures—was so familiar that my senses wrapped around it as naturally as a child holds an old ball. But my mind and heart were strangers to this place and this voice and I wanted to leave. I was afraid. Afraid that down deep in every one of us there may be something that even good will and love of truth cannot defend the human spirit against, if it grows too big. I was as terrified, for a moment, as if all the toy pistols and the matches had grown into atom and hydrogen bombs and smoking cities; as if this man's words, said now the magic number of times, had rubbed the lamp and brought forth the incredible event.

I felt, if I could only get to the next motor court, wherever it was, all would be well. But I was too tired to leave and it was much too late. I went to bed; and unable to sleep I lay there listening to the gator-frogs whose roar counterfeits the distant roar of an alligator so perfectly that it is difficult sometimes to distinguish between them. The sounds seemed so near. A monologue that went on and on. Frogs talking to themselves. . . . Keeping you out of the swamp when it's full of wonder, and danger too, of course; but there're flowers you find nowhere else in all the world, and long-winged slow-flying birds that sink into trees and close up into great clumsy buds, and thick entangling greenness, and cottonmouths, and gators squudging their way beneath water lilies—and panthers. What would a swamp be without a panther or two in it?

*But you must not go alone,* a grown-up voice said. *Never alone, remember! Then come with me, won't you,* a child was saying, *for I must see what is there.*

And now Susie and I were there—in Moscow—and Susie was carrying a pitcher of ice lemonade and a slice of marble cake to the Kremlin, looking for her last weary traveler. But there were so many, and all had to be questioned, and we could not decide who was the last one, really. For the Inquisitors had turned into little gator-frogs sitting around A Very Big Table, and they were roaring like jet planes—and you could not think, you could not decide anything. So we turned away and Susie wept because she could not carry out her Good Samaritan deed and now we were on a beach and all around us was Susie's loneliness and the only sound on earth was a music thin as a gull's cry that floated out of a starfish softly turning turning in wet sand and I knew I had heard it before but it was a cold sound to the heart—

I woke up, wet with sweat and chilled to the bone by the air conditioning. Turned off the noisy gadget. Went to the window. The stars looked just as they had when I went to bed (only the sky had slid over a little); just as they always had looked on a June night. Calm and sure, every star, every planet, and galaxy. Even the star dust was drifting neatly. Each star the exact number of millions of light-years away from us; each, in its place exactly as the physicists have charted it, moving in ancient orbit according to ancient rhythm. Some had reached their destination but they were still brightly shining—as if unaware that they had died. Everything seemed to be in fine order. If the end of time was near, apparently the universe had not yet been told. Only Susie. And then, the music sounded. I knew it now: a sonata of Bartok's and Menuhin's violin. . . .

Next morning, I went to see the tree. I did not want to see it. I wanted only to get away from this haunted place. But I went. I suppose I felt compelled to meet Susie, now that I had been to Moscow with her.

She turned as I walked up. I had circled the house and gone to the big tree, half hoping she would not be there. But she was there; very small and blank in its deep shadow. There were six great limbs, low to the ground, that spread wide black-green polished branches from end to end of the back yard and above them more limbs that lay heavy on the roof, and more and more that soared straight into the sky. And there were four thick roots that curved above white sand and plunged deep into the earth. It was truly a fabulous tree and for a moment I did not speak, so taken was I by its wonder.

"I was expecting you," she said gently. "Cephas told me you was acoming."

A face like wax. Eyes, big and unmoving, like a child's when listening to a story that must not end. Ageless eyes. Ageless face. Time had stopped for Susie. Even her body had guessed it for it was caught in amber-like stillness. One could not believe that under the yellowed smooth translucent skin a heart beat or blood moved even a slow inch. Only the hands, red, dry, from disinfectants and detergents, seemed in the living world for they looked as if they hurt.

"They're there, this morning," she said, "every last one of them. No use to listen, you won't hear them, they don't talk, they just play. Some have been in there since it was a little biddy tree and there's one over here who has been playing all by his-self nearbout eighty years on that same branch and two who have been—no, not there over here—sixty-four years, no sixty-three—Do you understand what I am saying?" she demanded with a fierce need to know.

"Yes," for I did. "It's the children, in the tree."

She smiled. "I might uv knowed you'd know. But Cephas can't see them. I keep trying to explain and when he won't even try to see them you can understand why I had to slap him, can't you?"

"Yes," I whispered.

"That was when they sent me away. You know, to that place."

"Yes," I whispered.

"They're fixing to send me back," Susie said sadly. "And I just don't want to go. Do you know what?"

"What?" I echoed.

"I'd as soon sharpen my nose on a sidewalk as go back to that place. Yes I would, just as soon."

"Maybe it will help you feel better, to go. Sometimes a hospital helps us."

Eyes, big, unmoving. "Only thing that can help me feel better is the end of time. And it's so long acoming. So long."

"Oh Susie," and now I was sharing her loneliness as completely as I had in the dream.

"If it would only come. Every sign is right but Cephas says it aint coming, that—But it is, it is. And when it comes I'll clap my hands and shout hallelujah and the voice of the seventh angel will begin to sound and the woman was given two wings of a great eagle that she might fly into the wilderness, into her place—" voice loud, singsonging now, "—where she is nourished for a time and times and half a time, from the face of the serpent—"

"Susie," I said, "maybe we'd better whisper. Those people in your nice clean rooms might wake up and if they wake up we can't stay here and watch the children. You wouldn't like to waken them, would you?"

"No." Voice like lead. "They must sleep sleep—"

She had forgotten the sleepers. "Aint they cute, the little boogers? Come over here—there's three of em bouncing on that limb—

"You know what?"

"What?" I echoed.

"She thinks I'll hurt *hers*." Voice like a briar. "Many a time I'd be real glad to baby-set but Grace says *No, she might hurt the kids*. She means *me*." She spat.

"Grace?"

"Jed's wife."

She was staring at the ground.

"If only it was a piece of glass," she whispered.

"What, Susie?"

"Cause if it was—" She shook her head.

"What, Susie?"

"If it was, then all of it would be together. You know!" Her voice was sharp.

"You mean we could see the whole tree, then?"

She smiled. "I might uv knowed he couldn't see it. You know what?"

"What, Susie?" I felt I would never escape her world now.

"I've never had no use for no man cep'n two in all the world. My daddy and God. The rest of em can just go and sharpen *their* noses—" She giggled and giggled and it truly was so merry that I loved laughing with her.

"Susie—" I touched her arm to quiet her, and felt nothing but a spindly bone there. "Susie," and I told her how much I had enjoyed the chicken and corn bread sandwich and the beautiful piece of marble cake. Then I said good-by. She ran quickly into the house. I turned to go back to the car but had not gone far when I heard her running behind me. She had brought me a little glass of mayhaw jelly. As I took it from her the sun touched it and a thousand red and yellow lights spilled out of it. "Look Susie, it is so pretty."

"Yes," she whispered, "everything is so pretty what people never see."

"Are you going a fur piece?" she asked as I started the motor.

"I'm looking for something," I told her, "that is very im-

portant to me to find. I am not quite sure how far I shall go
before I find it."

"Oh," she said, "bring it by and show me."

The car was moving slowly now. "Bring it by," she called.
And as I went down the highway her voice followed me:
*bring it by bring it by—*

Weak and small like the last cry for help of the medium's
daughter in Menotti's opera.

Soon, now, they will take her back to That Place. Yes. A
day will come when she will not have the strength or courage
or hope or desire to do her Good Samaritan deed another time—
and then? Then she may throw the lemonade in Cephas's face.
And they will come for her and take her so that she cannot
harm him or Grace's children, any more.

And Cephas? But I had to drive carefully here for a giant
Armour truck was passing a giant Swift truck and coming
behind me was a long silver Thing—now it was closer, a Greyvan full of somebody's furniture moving Home from one place
to another, and the driver signaled to pass—and suddenly my
Chevrolet seemed too small and insignificant to compete with
these giants. I had better take care. But I was unduly fearful for
they meticulously observed the traffic laws, and as the Greyvan
passed, the driver's assistant called out *Hi*—and now the three
giants were pulling off the road for breakfast at Ma's Kitchen.

And Cephas? The highway was deserted and cool and dim
now from the shadows thrown by the pine forest.

Each of us has our own secret language in which we call for
help. Perhaps that is why it is difficult to hear another's cry; or
even our own. Cephas could not hear Susie's small *help help,*

so plain to my ears. And I found it as hard, that morning, to hear his plea.

Cephas and Susie. . . . My unknown neighbors of childhood. Three children who lived close to the swamp, listening to the sounds, smelling the odors, looking at the sky, playing the games, asking the same questions.

Those hungry questions! They come out of a child's mind like little puppies, sniffing, tasting, trying out the world: *Where did I come from: Where am I going? Who is God? Tell me, tell me. When? where? why? why? why?* And then so slowly they change into *Tell me a story, won't you?* The human mind is learning to settle now for something smaller. If you cannot tell me the first and last chapters of my life, then tell me another story, almost anything will do—

Of course those questions could not be answered by our parents. And will never be answered completely by philosopher or scientist. But they are the way the child has of saying: *I want to know: I want to know everything about me, what draws me to you, what pulls us apart from each other. I want to know all about God. All about past and future. All about right and wrong. And everything about the earth and the sun and the moon and the stars and winter and summer and birds and ants and flowers and weeds and storms and beetles. I want to know what is inside the earth and what is inside me and what is inside my mother and what is inside a dream. And how far away the most distant star is and does a child live on it? I want to climb the peak that has never been climbed and swim in the biggest ocean and I want to go into the swamp. I want to know.*

"If only the ground was a piece of glass," cried Susie.

"Yes," echoes every child, "if I could only see the whole tree."

And what answers were given the hungry mind to grow on? Just a few scraps of half-lies and half-facts; and now and then wonderful ghost stories, or laughter, or silence. And finally slow-creeping shame submerged the questions. Shame for having been so silly as to want to know where you came from and where you are going and all about God. And much the same kind of answers were given the child who lived in a spacious house on College Street as was given the child who lived in a two-room cabin in the backwoods.

After a time the mind loses its hunger for truth if it is never fed it when young, and turns to strange substitutes as does the little clay-eater whose body, craving a balanced diet which it does not receive, develops an insatiable appetite for dirt.

I knew few facts about Susie's childhood or Cephas's. I knew a bit more about my own. And as I drove down the highway that day, past fine new factories and green-growing fields and fresh-painted houses, turning off now and then to find an old landmark of my family's past, I thought of those questions: the ones you asked, the ones you dared not put into words. And of Frashy's answers. For Frashy knew everything—even about Aunt Victoria, and babies and acorns. And how she loved to tell it!

## 9

I DO NOT remember my beautiful Aunt Victoria. Only the way she died. In our home it was of her, the living, that we heard. But Frashy and those Anonymous Others who have ready explanations for all human upheavals saw to it that her death would never be forgotten. They described the cough, the pallor, the swift wasting away of body as the galloping terror, Consumption, raced with her toward death. It was an appalling picture their words built up in my mind: a kind of montage of a Headless Horseman running down poor little Victy, of Paul Revere calling out that the enemy is here, of my older brother's horse who ran away with him once, and all the paintings of Albert Pinkham Ryder, and the illustrations in the big Bible upstairs in the library which pictured with ferocious relish the deaths and punishments that sinful mortals are subject to.

After explaining to us what it was, the informers told us *why*: It happened to people who had been bad when they were little; or whose family had been bad or whose grandparents had been bad; it—the sin—can go on to the second or third or fourth generation, one glib little schoolmate told me as we sat on the lawn on a fall day chewing sugar cane and eating boiled peanuts. She elaborated (her mouth full of sugar cane): It comes from most anything, from drinking and playing cards and saying bad words and cheating in school and running up debts and telling tales and stealing nickels and thinking things—*you know*, she underlined the words, and looked at me conspiratorily. Yes, I knew, heaven help me. Even at eight years old I believed I knew all about it.

My little schoolmates did their work well. But it was Frashy, the fifteen-year-old girl who tended my baby brother, who put on the finishing touches.

It was Frashy who also told us what happens if you swallow watermelon seeds. You swallow one of them seeds, said Frashy, and it'll lay in your stomach a while and then it'll sprout. It's dark down there and wet, so it'll grow all over the place and it'll come up through your gullet and out through your mouf and your nose and ears and it'll go up in your skull and crawl all around up there winding around your brain, and after a while it'll be such a vine that it'll trail everywheres, all over the place, trailing way behind you when you walks. And when it blooms—

—I bet it's real pretty when it blooms, I whispered, trying desperately to keep esthetic distance from this terror.

—Well, sometimes, Frash conceded reluctantly.

—But you wouldn't like it. She scowled and would not say more.

—Why?

—Because them vines would grow melons and them melons would be gittin bigger and bigger and then what you do with a dozen or so watermelons loading you down and catching on everything when you walk around? What you do then?

—I don' know, Frash.

—I tell you what you do. You lay down and die, that's what. So take them seeds out'n your mouf!

—And all we'd have to do, my brother shouted, to have a watermelon cutting would be to sit down and let everybody come with a big knife and slit the melons open. Shucks! Haw haw! He carefully spat the seeds out.

But I was so bemused by this image of myself trailing green vines into Sunday School and down to the drugstore to buy a sack of candy and sitting on the lawn while everybody had a watermelon cutting right off me, that I swallowed mine, and when I realized what I had done I screamed for an hour. My mother scolded Frashy and told me it was not true. But Frashy stood there rubbing her dip stick on her teeth and curled her lip just enough for me to know that my mother was wrong for Frashy *really knew*.

—Now if it's a acorn you swallow (Frashy loved to talk about swallowing things) it'll sprout a oak tree inside you and it'll grow too big to come out of your ears and nose and places so it'll just keep growing inside you, gittin bigger and bigger, and it'll keep pushing your skin out until nothing is left of you at all, not nothing. You'll jus be a piece of something like that there tissue paper yo birthday presents was wrapped in and pieces of yo skin will be hanging from the limbs of a big oak tree and when the wind blows, it'll rattle and sigh and all that goin-on will be you.

—Shucks, said my brother and threw away the acorn he had begun to nibble.

We knew about watermelons and oak trees growing inside people long before we knew where babies grew. But when my little brother was born—the last of the nine of us—Frashy explained that too.

She told us on the day he was born. It was a dramatic moment and Frashy had a delicate feeling for such occasions. She had been directed to keep us across the street at a neighbor's home but this was too far away from the center of things and Frashy felt it necessary, like the good reporter she was, to keep close to where headlines are made. So at the time of telling us, we were by some astute maneuvering of Frashy's sitting on our lawn, not far from the doctor's horse and buggy, and within earshot of the drama taking place within the house.

—Where is it coming from, Frash? My brother asked and the two of us watched her closely for we knew she was going to lie. But this fascinating game with Frashy was played on two levels. We loved her lies though they scared us to death. They made us have nightmares and sometimes lose our appetite for a week at a time and yet we begged for more. But though we honored our fifteen-year-old educator with a willingness to listen that few teachers in institutions have ever received, an edge of our young minds knew she was lying and we were determined to catch her at it. As we grew older, we did—so often that poor Frashy stopped talking. She'd just move her dip stick to the other side of her mouth and sull up and say I aint goin to tell you, you all talk back so and I don' like younguns who talk back. And so, she stopped telling us her stories. But we were older then. At this time, she still felt it her mission to brief us about life's big moments. And this was one of them.

—What coming? Frashy rolled her eyes.

—Where is it coming from, Frashy? I whispered.

Frashy rolled her eyes again and rubbed her front teeth, took her dip stick out of her mouth and looked at it. Reckon I'd better go git me a new one, she said.

—I'll git it for you, Brother said, but don't you tell Her until I come back.

Frashy sighed, slumped her shoulders, let her fingers play softly around the contour of her breast, held it there poised like a butterfly while I watched in deep fascination, sighed again. Brother was back with the twig he had pulled off the bush from which Frashy liked to get her dip sticks, and we were ready for the big lie.

—They come from different places, Frashy said slowly. Now if you lives close to a swamp, a gator might bring you.

—Shucks, said my brother, we live in town.

—Why you say that? Frash glared. You tell it, if you know so much!

—Go on, Frashy, I whispered.

—If you lives near a swamp, Ole Miz Gator might bring you. She'd keep you in a hole close to the edge of the pond with all her eggs and every day she go to the pond and swish-swash in and fill her big mouf with warm water and then she crawls back to her hole and squirts that water all over her eggs and all over you. How you like that? (She stopped her story and glared at us.) And when it's time for her eggs to hatch, she puts you on her back and comes to town and gives you to anybody who'll take you. For she got her own chillun to look after.

Frash had a real talent for making you feel cheap and rejected.

—And she take you to the back do' too for she shamed of yo looks.

And all the time we were letting Frashy lacerate our self-

esteem with these words, and urging her to do it, we knew that
the doctor's buggy was right there outside our gate and Aunt
Cynthia, the midwife, was inside the house at this minute and
our mother was in her big sunny bedroom. We knew this. And
we knew why. And yet we didn't know. It was a knowledge too
fleeting, too dark, too full of sounds without words. They were
bits of a mosaic but we dreaded the pattern that might be
there, were it put together. And we clung to Frashy's lies for
fear the truth would be more fabulous than we could bear.

And, of course, omniscient Frashy added an authority to the
Death of Aunt Victoria story which our schoolmates could not
match. She knew all about galloping consumption because she
had a friend who had just died of it. And it was because she
run off with a convict who'd walked out of the road camp. And
they laid out together in the woods, so Frashy told us, and then
they was caught and the folks she worked for let her go. And
then she run off with another man from the road camp—

—But Frash, why do people *have* consumption?

It was no use.

. . . another man, and he left her and then she died of the
consumption. And that is what yo aunt died of and you got
the same puny look.

—Is it in the blood, Frash?

—All meanness is in the blood, silly! And you sho must ter
had some mean folks in yo family if you and Brother is the best
they could do.

We were used to her insults and paid no more attention than
to the mosquitoes. But it worried us, nevertheless, this sin in the
blood. For our father at family prayers, now and then, read that
line: *The sins of the fathers . . . even unto the third and fourth*

*generation,* and always when he did, I thought of poor beautiful
Victy who had to die for great-great-grandfather's sins. Now I
do not think my father deliberately chose the passage. He
believed the reading of the Scriptures, any portion of it, was
an ennobling experience for readers and listeners—especially
for children. And because he was a busy man and felt he must
hurry down to the office at the mill as quickly as possible in the
mornings, he found it easy to open the Holy Book and read
whatever page his eyes lighted upon. Sometimes this habit of
his gave an immense zest to family prayers. There was the time
he began to read about Lot and his daughters and then seeing
what he was in for, he skipped over and landed in the middle of
a lush passage from the Song of Solomon. (Mother, the
only efficient censor in our family, was rarely at the table to
help my father through his editorial troubles. She was usually
in the kitchen helping the cook take up breakfast, for it was no
small feat to serve a family of eleven and often more—for one
grandmother was usually with us and cousins came and went,
and if a Methodist preacher was passing through town he
always spent the night in our home, and even the tramps who
came down to Florida for the winter were invited to sit at our
table if they happened by at breakfast time, for my father
believed a man who needed food needed more than do other
mortals to have that food served him with dignity and grace.)

I am sure that whatever he read from the Bible—whether
alarming or highly instructive—he read with innocence. But
we children never heard that armored phrase, *the sins of the
fathers,* without looking quick at Little Grandma to see if she,
too, saw Victy run over by it. But always her face was serene and
quiet, and my father's voice was firm and sure, and it was diffi-

cult to believe that such words could be relevant to our family.
But I was not sure ... and I tried now and then to ask Little
Grandma why Victoria had to die for the family's sins and what
those sins were but I could never quite do it for I could not have
borne it had those clear brave eyes suddenly darkened, even for
a moment, with hurt and guilt. I hushed my question, but now
and then when alone, I wondered and shivered at my thoughts.
And at these defenseless times, I would remember the bits which
Frashy had handed out in her effort to dominate our minds.

And yet, she did not scare us too much. Frash was our substitute for today's comic books and headlines. And, like them,
could not long win the credulity of a moderately informed
human being. But, like those comic books and headlines, the
incredible bits, the things your conscious mind refused even
when you were six years old, were just the same pushed back
with the rest: with the blind boy who had once lived in our
town and could not see, they said, because somebody had done
something bad before he was born; and with the day (in a town
fifty miles away where each summer my sister and I visited
relatives) when a playmate took us to her parents' big old house
and whispering that on the third floor they kept their aunt who
was a "lunatic," she slipped us up the back stairs and let us peek
in the window at that poor distraught woman. And that, too,
had happened because God had to punish somebody (though
He seemed always to be punishing the wrong somebody). And
there was Carl—and all the children who died every summer—

And there was more. Had there not been, perhaps these bits
of fantasy and half-lies and quarter-truths might have sifted out
of our memory. But they were held there by experiences more
deeply felt because closer to our bodies and closer to those we

loved and longed to please. One of these I shall tell here, a small story, about three children:

They had been hunting for doodlebugs. (You chant *doodle-bug, doodlebug, come come come, your house is on fire and your children burning up*, then you stick a straw down one of the holes which dot the sand, hoping for that fine moment when up comes a doodle.)

But after a time, nature proved imperative and the three playmates trotted off to the "garden house" which was set behind the rose trellis—a process which diverted their interests from doodlebugs to the beguiling area of their bodies. In her attempt to fasten her small panties to an underwaist studded with double rows of buttons (these were old-fashioned times) Little Sister was forced to call on the two small boys for assistance. On the path leading back to the house, the three struggled with the buttons.

A bumblebee came along, buzzed at the little girl and she promptly dropped the panties. On warm days she wore a pinafore and this was tied now around her waist.

Brother said slowly, "I don' look like you."

Playmate said, "I sho don' neither."

Bumblebee was forgotten.

"Show me how you look!" Imperiously.

The small boys obeyed. The three stared thoughtfully.

Little Sister said, "He's black."

Playmate grinned. "Sho."

"Sho he's black," Brother affirmed.

Then Little Sister made a discovery. "Both of you is just like Strophanes, Junior." Aristophanes Junior being Uncle John's dog.

The two boys checked carefully. There was no doubt about it. "You aint," Brother bragged.

Little Sister shook her head disconsolately, "No, I aint."

Their tactful playmate searched for a morsel of encouragement. "Maybe you is like. . . ." To tell the truth, he didn't know, but now slowly, unemotionally, with the concentration which served them well in their play they were off on the search for knowledge.

Playmate had it. "Maybe you is like a hen."

Little Sister's lip trembled, "I tan't lay no egg."

"No, she can't," Brother admitted reluctantly.

It was imperative to find something that she was like, for a storm was working up as anyone with half an eye could see.

Playmate tried again. "Maybe she's like Peggy." Peggy was the old carriage horse, soon to be retired to the pasture.

The other two frowned. Maybe so. They weren't sure. Playmate, with inexorable logic: "They've both got ladies' names."

"That's so," said Brother.

"And they don' look like us."

"No they don't."

"Then they must be alike."

"Yeah."

"Is Anthony like me, too?" Little Sister's aspirations had begun to soar. Anthony was her big brother's beautiful saddle horse.

Playmate didn't know. But Brother remembered.

"No," he said, "Anthony aint like you a bit."

"Is he like you?"

"Yeah."

"Then horses is girls and boys."

The boys nodded carelessly. It was totally new and fascinating knowledge but the final deduction had come from a girl and must be accepted casually.

And now they began to explore the animal kingdom:

"Does dogs always look like us?"

Playmate, "I reckon they do."

"An' cats?"

If dogs did, then cats did.

"n' cows"

"n' bulls"

"Yeah—n' polecats."

The problem in biology was dwindling now as the old game of words speeded up:

"n' elephants"

"n' giraffes"

"n' camels"

"n' monkeys"

"n' lions"

"n', n',"—but they had reached the outer edge of the circus parade world.

"and—and—" Brother was lost.

"and—and—baboons," Playmate yelled.

"and doodlebugs," Sister shrieked.

"No, suh," Brother shouted decisively, "not doodlebugs."

"No, suh, not doodlebugs," reinforced Playmate.

Little Sister looked from one to the other. The masculine world had again aligned itself against her. She let the tears fill her eyes but she refused to be downed. "Why?"

Brother stared at her. "Jus—jus because," doggedly.

Tears swimming now. "Tell me why."

Playmate stared at her. "Dat's right, jus because."

"I know they is. I'll ask Mama." Indignant sob.

They knew she would.

"No you can't! Can't ask your mama that." Playmate's voice had no shred of tact in it now.

"Why?"

"Sho can't talk to grown folks about that."

"Why?" She turned to Brother.

"Cause he says you can't." Settled.

"Then why not doodlebugs?" challengingly.

Playmate thought hard. Then he smiled ingratiatingly, "Cause they's way too little."

"Oh," said Sister, believing herself convinced.

Sweat was streaming down their faces for the day was blazing hot but Sister's voice plodded on. "Den worms—"

"Nope."

"Nope," echoed Playmate.

And then it happened. Frashy saw them, and with a *law hep me* she dashed in to tell their mother. She had been waiting for a week to find something to tell on them, to get even with them for hiding from her when she called them to meals. And this was it.

"What on earth does this mean?" Brother looked up blankly into his mama's pale face. But Playmate knew from something in his experience that a mighty bad time was ahead for everybody and it was sure to be worse for him than for anybody else.

She turned to little playmate. "Go at once to Aunt Susan." (Aunt Susan was the cook and their playmate was her little grandson.)

"Now," after the small thing had lit out like a streak of

lightning, "what were you doing?" Voice low and stern, she addressed her words to Brother.

"Playing animals."

"Playing animals?" Their mother was puzzled. "Why have you no clothes on?"

In surprise Brother looked at his nakedness. As usual, the beginning of the game was forgotten. "I—I—" then he remembered, "we was showing each other how we looks."

She knelt beside her children. The Stern Parent in this kind sensitive woman had now taken over. The Parent believed it must be said and she said it: "Listen to me, both of you, and never forget this as long as you live. The body is bad and must never be looked at. Do you understand? You must never look. Only vulgar people look at each other's bodies. And you must never talk about it. To each other or to anyone. You—," she hesitated as she turned to her little son, "you didn't—touch her, did you?"

Brother's sweaty lips began to tremble, "No mam."

"Did—he?"

"No mam."

She quickly dressed Sister. "I should switch you both. I know I should. For you have done almost the worst thing a little boy and girl can do. But I am not going to." (It would have been for her an almost impossible duty.) "I know my children will never do such a thing again, will they? Never talk about such things again. Mama wants them to be good and clean, more than she wants anything else in the world. She loves you—it would break her heart—"

The children were sobbing violently now, terrified by the anguish in their mother's face.

She led them to the house, each clinging tightly to one of her hands. They could not have borne it, had they not those hands to hold to.

As they went down the path they heard sharp screams from Playmate who had been conveyed to the privacy of Aunt Susan's little house in the back yard for a good thrashing, for the tattling girl had rushed triumphantly with the disgrace to this dignified old lady in the kitchen who now did her duty to her grandson as she and her employer saw it.

And then Little Grandma came out. She had heard. Enough to know. Enough to show her sympathy to her daughter-in-law by the softness in her voice. Enough to take the children for the rest of the morning.

"Now what do we want to play?" she said, and took them and their sin on her lap, warming with her acceptance their shivering little souls on this hot summer day.

"A-a-bout the pan-panther," said Brother, swallowing his sobs.

"Y-y-y-yes mam," gasped Sister, "t-t-tell us a-about the panther."

And there was Playmate at the door sniffing and wiping his nose and Little Grandma called him, and he sat down beside her and put his hands on her knee and said, "Y-y-yes, Little Grandma, p-please mam, t-tell us about the panther."

So it goes. . . . The little things, the silence and the laughter and the shame, the comic book stories, the Frashy lies, the whispers of schoolmates and words from the Bible, too, and the headlines, and a demagogue's loud words, creep close to these deeper hurts in our lives. And all of it is swept up behind rows and rows of fine modern gadgets that trick us into believing we have modern minds. And then, one day, the wind blows and with sudden startling force the present is filled with these dusty distortions, blinding us so that we have no idea which way the future lies.

Unless—

The air was heavy now with the scent of a paper mill. I was nearing St. Marys. Once this small and very old town was an important harbor in the pre-Civil War plantation days, then it shriveled into a little fishing village where shrimp boats anchor in the evenings. Now, today, it is the home of a big mill, and of government projects.

—unless, when one is young, one learns to love the truth.

Nowhere, as I wandered under those ancient oaks did I see a sign of my mother's past. I was not sure, even, where the old place had been up the river. Where could I find roots here? It seemed as if my learned old grandfather and the knowledge he loved had never existed, so completely were all signs of him gone.

And then, I thought of our "library." It was a room his daughter and son-in-law had set aside in their home. And though Grandfather had rarely been in that house after I was born— for he died when I was very young—the room was there because his love of books was something that my parents felt must stay in their home. A little Shrine to Truth—not untarnished, I fear, but always there.

The old room . . . I could see it as I stood on the pier watching a shrimp boat come in across the harbor. Upstairs it was, and large and rambling; built on two levels and with many windows. It was half library and half "company room." The visiting Methodist preachers always slept in it. And above the

mantel was a portrait of Susanna Wesley in a terrifying cap.
(I don't know what my Catholic-bred grandfather thought of
Susanna.) When I was small I believed that she stayed in the
picture frame only when my parents did not need her help
downstairs. The rest of the time, she was invisibly but most
efficiently overseeing our "discipline." My father believed in
Susanna Wesley's knowledge of children as ardently as modern parents, today, believe in Gesell.

In the bay window was a desk and on the wall opposite
were the books. Only a few hundred of them and as odd an
assortment of truth and error as one would be likely to come
across in print. My grandfather's books were not here. Vicissi-
tudes of war, reconstruction, migration from one town to another and Big Grandma's carelessness (I fear) had scattered
them. Perhaps it is just as well that the old gentleman never
knew this and never saw the shrine our family had set up so
lovingly in his memory. For it contained the sermons of Dwight
L. Moody, and of DeWitt Talmadge; and the far more exciting
sermons of Sam Jones and a few other old fire-and-brimstone
evangelists (all of which I had read before I was eleven years
old). There was a book called *In His Steps* and two terrifying
books on Hell, and an illustrated Bible and Burton's *Anatomy
of Melancholy.* (Mother's "doctor book" which I discovered in
her bedroom closet was not here, of course, but it too mixed
inextricably with these others in my mind.) And of course
there were *Pilgrim's Progress* and *Robinson Crusoe* and *Gul-
liver's Travels.* Side by side with these, were Dante and Shakespeare and Goethe and the *Canterbury Tales*; a complete set of
the novels of Oliver Wendell Holmes; and George Eliot;
Dickens, Thackeray, Mark Twain, Victor Hugo; and almost

every English poet from Spenser to Browning; there were Emerson and Thoreau, Poe and Hawthorne (these two my mother loved). I cannot remember all the titles but I had read all the books again and again before I completed high school.

For a time came, in those young years, when I grew skeptical of my schoolmates' explanations and of Frashy's big lies and of the silence of grownups. The old questions were hurting again. I was longing for "the truth" as I had hungered for it when two, three, four years old—only now, I asked the questions in different words, and did not go to people for the answers. I began to make purposeful trips to that upstairs room. Then it was, that I found Shakespeare. The summer I was twelve I read all his plays in one big gulp, for a child greedy for experience reads as she devours candy.

Were my questions answered? I don't know. I forgot them. I was translated into a new world: a place where no man is The Stranger however different his experience of life may be. Those amazing, ambient words pouring out of the deeply accepting mind and heart of The Poet had metamorphosed everyone on earth, overnight, into a human being: fascinating, real, mysterious, tender, and terrifying, and awesome, and funny, and ordinary—and so like one's self.

. . . *and the Word was God.*

I understood now, a little. Just a little. But enough never to forget that when the search for truth is held cheap, the search for God is held cheap also; and then, Man made in His image becomes only an object to be used like a Thing for one's own greedy purpose.

I understood; not in words but in feelings. There were no words in me for a long time after reading Shakespeare. I went around like a little mute, deaf to everything but the feelings the poet had left in my mind.

Where had I come from? And where was I going? Those old questions would come back, someday. But now, I no longer cared: I was so glad to be here.

It was not long after this great wealth had tumbled into my head that I discovered Bach and Beethoven and Chopin and Schumann (and a few others, of course, as odd as the old dusty authors in our library) for there was a music teacher. And she was, for me, the Good Teacher.

And Susie and Cephas? For them?

No books, no little shrine to truth, no music teacher. In that small backwoods cabin crowded by poverty and isolation there was no room for them.

That is not quite right. Susie had her Bible and she learned Revelations by heart. And she had her magnolia tree. And out of these she made her "grass harp" and learned to play it all by herself, and to do her little Good Samaritan deed every Sunday. And Cephas learned to play a harp of fire, and to make the money he had never had which he thought would bring him something more modern than truth and finer than a human being.

All day, as I drove along, I thought of them. Sometimes hearing Susie playing. Sometimes Cephas. Sometimes, all of us playing . . . all of us, playing our harps. . . .

What eerie and thunderous and strange and lovely music we make as we try to teach our terrors to sing.

## ৩ 10 ৪

"I was in the fifth grade," he said, "and Miss Molly was the new teacher. Most of us were children of sharecroppers. All were poor—except Cynthia. Her father owned the biggest cotton farm in the county. The school was a two-room school, three miles away. Of course we walked. The teacher, too.

"She was round as an apple and as pretty and smelled as good. There were thirty-five or forty of us in her room. She taught five grades, did her own janitoring, stoked the stove—and told us the most wonderful stories a boy ever listened to."

About China and India and Africa; Paris and London, Florence, Peking, Cairo; about subways and elevated trains; and great art museums; and waterfalls and the big rivers of the earth and deserts and oceans. She brought them all into that unpainted schoolhouse and its walls stretched like rubber.

One day, Miss Molly took them across a desert. "How we sweated that day. The glare was terrific. But we went right on, Miss Molly leading the way. We scorched our feet on sands hotter than any sand could ever be in Georgia, lost a slow-poke around the sand dunes but he caught up with us; saw a mirage

in the sky, thirsted for water, ate dates, searched for an oasis—
and found one just as the sun went down. We rested there
while purple and black and green-blue lights streaked the sands.
And then, suddenly, we were back in the schoolhouse and Miss
Molly gave us colored chalk and we drew pictures of what
we had seen.

"Another time, we spent the night at the foot of the Sphinx.
We rode on camels, went to the tombs, and stayed all night to
watch the sun rise in Egypt.

"Once, we were in Peking. We got in rickshas and although
we knew (because she told us) that only one person rode in a
ricksha, she let two of us ride together because we were sort of
lonely way out there in China. We jog-jogged out to the Temple
of Heaven. And all the way, the ricksha coolies talked in their
quick sharp Chinese words to each other and we could not
understand; we just watched the red glow of the lanterns hanging from the ricksha. And then, suddenly, we were there. And
moonlight was everywhere. We climbed those white glistening
marble steps of the Altar of Heaven and stood, with Miss Molly,
looking at Man's dream carved in stone. And back of us was
the temple roof, curving against the sky. . . . And she told us
about Confucius, and the Golden Mean, as we stood there.

"And do you know, I found out after I was grown that Miss
Molly had never been out of Georgia."

The children would sit in those rough desks spellbound. "To
tell you the truth, I'm not sure there were desks, for I vaguely
remember benches and the back of my legs hurting."

Miss Molly could pull time back and forth like syrup
candy. "One day, when we got to school, time had slid back
a million years and she told us all day long about what was

happening on earth: the dinosaurs had died but the ants were still here, the pterodactyls had gone but the horse was coming along fine—and she ended up with the last Ice Age beginning to melt and Man beginning to emerge."

"Ever have time for arithmetic and spelling?"

"In between journeys. We learned it fast so we could get back to discovering things.

"Another day, it would be yesterday that she talked about; and we'd hear what was happening in the world now. Not one of our parents, except Cynthia's, took a newspaper."

Miss Molly had a pair of field glasses. Once, after she had been home she brought back a borrowed telescope and a microscope. Every two or three weeks, they had a box supper at the school and would look through the telescope at the stars.

There were parents who did not like this. "How you know what those younguns are up to, out there in the black dark." Some said Miss Molly must not know what was in the books or else she wouldn't be so interested in things outdoors.

"She told us the life history of the frog. I didn't dare tell my folks we were learning about tadpoles. And the other kids knew better than to tell it either for we feared Miss Molly might disappear. Grown folks could do things like that to your teacher.

"She taught us only one year. I've never known whether the grown folks sent her away or whether she went to a bigger schoolhouse."

"Where did she come from?"

"A little town about forty miles away. She went back there, after she retired from teaching, and ran her old father's general merchandise store until she died, last year."

"An extraordinary person."

"You know," he puffed on his pipe, looked at a Klee print in their small attractive coffee shop where we were sitting, smiled at his wife, Ellen. "I am not sure there was anything extraordinary about Miss Molly, except what she could do to children's minds. She was the best teacher I have ever heard of because she took nothing on earth or in the heavens or in a human being for granted. It was headline news to Miss Molly when a butterfly hatched out, or a new question hatched in your mind, or you found a bug you had never seen before. And there would be more news tomorrow. We knew it, as we picked up our lunch pails and tablets and geography books to go back to those little unpainted shacks we called home, and not one of us aimed to miss it."

"One day, she told us about college. I had never heard the word."

It was quite a story: Miss Molly began in the Dark Ages. She told them of Greece, of Egypt and Assyria, India and China where men had found much wisdom and knowledge about themselves and their world and had recorded it carefully, writing it down, engraving it in stone, painting pictures, making poems and great pieces of sculpture. But Rome had now fallen. And fear and hate lay heavy on the people. There was much suffering and disease swept across the land like a forest fire, until finally the people were cut off from all that men had learned to treasure of what they knew and thought about themselves and the earth.

"Miss Molly built up the darkness and the ignorance until we shivered with terror. Then she lit a candle." She told them about men called scholars, and men called monks, cloistered in small rooms in cold monasteries made of stone, who spent their

time carefully writing down with a quill pen all they knew, all
they could get hold of, of the past's great learning. She showed
them pictures. And then she told them of illuminated manuscripts. "Until I was in college," Timothy said, "an illuminated
manuscript had, in my mind, a nimbus above it."

"And then came the Renaissance. And suddenly the Greek
poets and the Latin poets were rediscovered; great thinkers
began to ask great questions, and soon, scientists began to find
out important facts about the universe nobody had known before. And the Powers grew angry. For while they were half-
willing for old knowledge to be treasured, they feared new
knowledge and began to burn men who discovered new facts
or thought new ideas. They were Inquisitors," Miss Molly said
severely.

"We got terribly excited. It seemed just like a lynching. Then
she told us about a wonderful man who had fallen in love with
human intelligence. His name was Day Car." Timothy spelled
it for me, eyes twinkling. "To think is of all man's achievements, the greatest, Miss Molly told us. And she had those
little ragged, half starved children repeat together: *I think,
therefore I am.* Then she told us Day Car said it.

"From that day, I was all for Day Car. I'd go fishing at the
pond and along would come Day Car. And we'd carry on conversations. He was my constant companion. When I came across
Descartes at college, well, he never seemed quite as wise a man,
nor quite as reliable a friend as old Day."

Then it was—after she had brought them in her own way
through the Dark Ages and the Renaissance, the Reformation
and the beginning of science—that Miss Molly built up the idea
of *college*. She told these children about the great universities

of Italy and Spain, about Oxford, Cambridge, and Heidelberg. As she told it, *college* was a sanctuary; and a repository for all the knowledge of our human past; and a great laboratory, too, in which scientists were discovering new facts about the universe and proving them; and where they worked in peace for nobody ever thought of hurting them in the sanctuary. And there were thousands of books at college, and professors, and beautiful green grass, and great trees and always a pipe organ, and people there were proud that they were human and could think.

Then she said, How many of you would like to go to college? And every child in the room held up a hand.

But only a few got there.

One of the girls made it. "How in the world Lizzie did it, I don't know. Her family was as poor as mine and set against Miss Molly because she had told us the earth was millions of years old—which made her against the Bible, they said."

"The others?"

"Two more of us got there. Not everybody's father was a sharecropper but nobody's family in that room had an income in those bad times of more than three or four hundred dollars a year. Except Cynthia's. Nice girl, Cynthia. Used to give somebody a share of her lunch every day. Rest of us had cold biscuit with a hole punched in it and filled with syrup."

"My mind nearly burst open that day. I couldn't wait to get home to tell Mommie and Pap."

His mother was toting the slops to the hog pen. He followed her and talked about college while the hogs grunted and fought each other over the slops and the smells rose up and enveloped them. As he talked, he took a stick and opened up a little ditch so some of the water could drain out. "To this day, I see

that water trickling out of the pen. Funny—things the memory
holds to." But his mother didn't seem to understand and just
stared at the hogs and interrupted to ask him to go draw her
a pail of water for the kitchen. When she came in, she sat
down to catch her breath. He lit the kerosene lamp. Its light
lay plain on the spreading sore on her face and he knew his
mother hurt too bad for him to talk to her.

"I remember I suddenly grew afraid to tell my dad. And yet
I felt compelled to do it."

Pap was washing his feet in a tin pan on the front porch.
He always said nothing hurt him but his feet; after plowing all
day, they weren't worth two cents.

"I told him about college: the monks and the scholars, the
illuminated manuscripts, and the inquisitors, and Day Car. And
he worked that washrag in between his toes, from big toe to
little toe, and didn't say a word. But I knew he was listening.
Then I told him about Oxford and Cambridge and Heidelberg;
about the books and the professors and the grass and the pipe
organ. And that we had colleges in America, too, thousands of
them started by the Pilgrim Fathers and the Quakers and the
Methodists—and every state in the Union, I said proudly, had
some. They're everywheres, Pap, I told him."

Pap dried his feet slowly. He said, "Tim, throw the water
out, won't you?" And Timothy ran out with the pan and
threw the water close to the cannas for his mother thought it
helped them grow.

When Timothy came back Pap was looking down at his feet.
He studied them a while and then he said, "Has the Baptists
got one, Tim?"

Tim told him the Baptists had them, too.

Pap studied a while longer. Then he looked up, said, "I reckon you better go, Son."

So Timothy went to college. He started that evening but it was a long time before he got there. His mother died the next year. Cynthia's father found a place for him to live with a family in town where he could go to school. He got in the wood and kept the yard cleaned for his board. Later the Baptist Church helped him secure a scholarship, he found a job waiting on tables. "And finally, I went to that Baptist college where my father wanted me to go." He laughed. "It wasn't exactly like Oxford and Heidelberg but there was a pipe organ and plenty of trees and grass—and far more books than I dreamed could ever be stacked in one big room, and, well, it looked pretty good to a country boy."

And as he talked, I could hear Cephas saying *Then burn em. Burn em all up.* And Susie whispering, *If the ground was only a piece of glass.* And I told Timothy and Ellen about them: about Cephas and his mauve bathroom fixtures and his "mod-run" motor court and Susie's tree full of ancient children, and her Good Samaritan deed. And we talked of the wondrous and terrifying ways by which men defend themselves from their fears, and of the ingenious and sometimes faltering ways in which they bind themselves to their world.

I had arrived during the afternoon at their motor court. He was at the desk. Freckled face, red hair climbing away from his brow, and big knuckly sunburned freckly hands. Voice easy, clean-chiseled. I signed the guest card, and looked for something to read. The usual things were in the rack. Under a rental clip were the N. Y. *Herald Tribune Books*, the N. Y. *Times*

*Book Review*, the London *Times and Literary Supplement*. A stand of paper books for sale. Two shelves of books for rent. The first titles I read were Eliot's *Four Quartets* and *Murder in the Cathedral*. Books of short stories by Eudora Welty, Katherine Mansfield, and A. E. Coppard. Toynbee's *A Study of History*. Haniel Long's *Letter to St. Augustine*. Rolfe Humphries' poems. Dostoevski's *The Idiot*. Faulkner's *Light in August*. Thomas Wolfe's books. Barnett's *The Universe and Dr. Einstein*. Sandburg's *Lincoln*. Martin's *The Meaning of a Liberal Education*. Lawrence's *The Rainbow*. Williams' *The Glass Menagerie*. There were more.

"Your rental books are rather unusual," I had said.

He smiled. "They are mine and my wife's personal books. Since we liked them enough to buy them, we think perhaps others may like them too."

There were three Rouault prints hanging in the office. In the hall, two or three prints of Kaethe Kollwitz's drawings.

We talked briefly about the prints and they told me they changed them each month. Last month, Marin's water colors were up. The month before Cézannes.

I asked them where they had met each other.

"At college. Ellen had never known poverty, until she knew me; her family were rich, mostly in human kindness but they had material things too."

"Not much. Tim exaggerates, a little."

But it looked like a lot to Tim. So much, that he had been afraid to marry her. Things, suddenly, became important to him—when he saw the big house in which her family lived and the fine old furniture and the silver and linens and expensive car. Her parents had invited him to visit them. He was given the guest room. A beautiful room with French windows and a private bath and a fine old mahogany fourposter and a cherry highboy—"and I don't know what all. That night I slept on percale sheets. The first I'd ever seen. I lay there stretched out on that smoothness and thought, So this is what it means to be rich. Pretty nice, huh? I meant to laugh. But I was crying. Like a big fool of a baby I cried for an hour. I cried first because my mother had not slept on any sheets at all most of her life; when she had, it was a piece of unbleached muslin over a cornshuck mattress. I cried because Ellen had always slept on fine percale sheets and I was afraid I could never make enough money to sleep with her on them." He winked at Ellen.

And he cried because all that Miss Molly had taught him to love and to want to know began to shrink in the presence of things, things, things. Maybe Miss Molly should have taught them how to make money, how to hunger and thirst for it, instead of teaching them to want to know about dinosaurs and the Altar of Heaven, and time and space, and the human soul. "I hated her. Everything began to go to pieces inside me. I began to do damfool things like saying, 'Your friend's house must have cost a pretty penny. $50,000, maybe?' And Ellen would just say she didn't know. And I'd say, 'Now that car there—you needn't tell me! It's a Cadillac. At least I can read.' See, I got ugly and vulgar. Then I began to think, Maybe the socialists *have* got something after all. I read Marx. I spouted *Das Kapital* for weeks. I read Veblen. Oh yeah, I was an expert now about the class conflict and ready to join up with almost anything.

"Another time, when I was visiting them, I said to Ellen's mother, 'That's a mighty fine old table. Must have cost a lot.'

And bless her, she said in her quiet kind voice, 'I love it very much, Tim. My grandfather made that table out of two old apple trees in his father's field.'

" 'A hobby?' I asked, and my voice was mean.

" 'In a way,' she said." And she told him:

Her grandfather was a blacksmith. At night, because he was a country boy and loved to whittle and work with wood, he made it for his wife. It took him two years to finish it the way he wanted it. It was the only pretty thing they ever had. And they cared enough to take it through a flood out in Ohio and a war down here in the South and their children cared enough to bring it along with them through hard times when for years it seemed as if they needed a lot of things more than an apple-wood table. "But you see, Tim, something in them did need that little applewood table. So they held on. It was my mother's. She gave it to me when I was a little girl."

"I hushed. I really shut my mouth."

"Yeah," he said after we had sat there a long time listening to the rain, listening to home, each of us drawn far away from that motor court by a different voice, "I sort of understand Cephas. Because I was worse. I had known something better than money. Cephas never has. But when I came close to money for the first time, I lost my head—worse than Cephas. I wanted it or else I didn't want anybody else to have it. Terrible feeling. I'm not sure what word fits it." He wrinkled his brow, sucked on his pipe—got up, went to the door, looked out at the storm. Came back.

"Awe. That's it. I felt an awe for Things That Cost Money. I could not find their place in my life. It was far easier to worship them, or else be an ascetic and reject them and all money, than it was to work out a human relationship with them. I had to find the delicate point of equilibrium where they can serve the human spirit—not destroy it. And it's in a different place in every one of us. I would never have found it, had it not been for Ellen, and her parents—and an artist named Lamar Dodd."

"Tim," said Ellen, smiling to keep the tears back, "it is very easy for you to be the villain in the piece, isn't it?"

He stared at her solemnly, ran his fingers through his hair, and laughed. "Yes. Because I still feel guilty. It took me too long to learn.

"Why her parents tolerated me five minutes, I still don't see!" Ellen's father was the doctor in a small town; and owned the drugstore. One day, he asked Tim to go with him out in the country where he was going to deliver a baby. As he drove along, he talked. Easy. "As if he had a half-crazy patient on his hands," said Timothy. He said money seemed to him like a powerful chemical. You've got to have a little of it to be healthy and human, and not only you but everybody's got to have it, to keep epidemics of disease and war and hate from sweeping across the world. But a lot of it may kill you. More than you need is sure to harm you unless you can get rid of it. And you can't get rid of it, he said, even if you give all of it away, if you still hunger and thirst for it. If you really care for it, you're as lost as an alcoholic. The thirst comes from pretty much the same trouble inside you, he said.

"He was driving a Model T. Said nothing could go through clay like a Model T and he had plenty of clay to go through.

He told me a man can pile up a lot of things around him in a lifetime. But if he begins to care too much for them they'll lock together and he'll be shut in a prison he can't get out of."

Ellen's father had been a poor boy. Not as poor as Tim; but too poor to dream of being a doctor. Why the desire had come, he never was sure. But from the time he was fourteen, he thought of nothing else. He had to make sick folks well. He'd go in to old Dr. Simpson's office and stare at that picture of the physician by the sick child's bed. The old country doctor watched him one day for a long time, then called him in and talked to him. And when he was grown, he helped him get to medical school. Lent him the money. Took him around with him in his buggy in the summer. Showing him. Teaching. "Somebody always helps you," Ellen's father told Tim. "You had your Miss Molly and a lot of others, maybe. I had old Dr. Simpson. You never do it alone.

"When I married Ellen's mother, she had money," the doctor said. "Not much, when you think of really rich folks. But it seemed a lot to me. And I lost my head. Made as big a fool of myself as you're doing now," he said. "Funny—no, it's damned sad to think that I measured my dream against her old dad's bank account and thought what I had to offer was no good. I began to think of getting rich off my patients; maybe go to the city; let country folks look after themselves. I began to cater to the well-known families. I broke my heart and hers before I learned my lesson. If you haven't got something better to offer a woman than a bank account, Tim—you're not going to satisfy her."

"He gave me the facts of life that day," said Timothy. " 'If what you value, the dreams you have are worth anything you hold on to them. If the woman you love doesn't value them, then she ain't worth it. That's all. But I think you're underrating my daughter.'" Tim laughed. "He glared at me as if he could cut my throat."

The learning was slow. "I got where I didn't bow and scrape every time I saw a big car or a fine house; and I stopped spouting *Das Kapital*. But I still found Fifth Avenue windows too damned impressive on my trips to New York. And still gawked when I saw the little heifers—as our old sharecropping neighbor would have called them—all swaddled up in their mink, stepping out of Twenty-One.

"But thank God, that applewood table haunted me. I'd lie awake at night, not often but now and then, thinking about two apple trees blooming in an orchard far away in Ohio. Sometimes they were as still as if they were frozen. Other times, a wind would be spraying the blossoms every which-a-way. And the next time, maybe, when I thought about them, those two trees would be loaded with apples, and the autumn sky shiny blue and the air coldish warm, and they'd smell sweet and good, like Miss Molly. And then, again, I'd see them: old and gnarled, blooming a little but just enough for Ellen's great-grandmother to have a spray or two for her pitcher—and only a handful of apples would mature, kind of nubby now but winy sweet. Then one time, I saw the trees cut down. A few boards were sawed up. And he, The Man (for he had no other name in my mind), had begun to make something pretty for his wife.

"I'd think about it as I fished; or out duck shooting; once during an examination when I was working for my Master's degree. It had something important to tell me, only I could not understand its language. I'd see The Man fitting the pieces of wood together; rubbing them smooth; carving the legs and smoothing the edges, holding the wood up to the light now and then; working on it, evening by evening, whittling, rubbing, until it had become a real and enduring experience: this wood and the hours he spent with it.

"One night I thought: That's it. He has a relationship now with it; as real as mine with my old friend, Day. Out in the orchard he had admired those trees, played in their branches, eaten the apples. But they were trees. And he was a boy. But now, something had happened between him and that wood. He had laid his dream on it; shaped it with his hands into something that makes human life sweet and good. And then he died. As the trees had died. But the table lived on. And the woman he loved, died; and the applewood table lived on. And their daughter died and the little table was still there.

"I found out something else: The Man had made it because he loved a woman; but he made it because of another reason, also.

"And I didn't know what that reason was. I nearly drove Ellen's folks crazy. For I'd go sit and stare at that applewood table, trying to put it all together in my mind. *Something in them needed that table,* Ellen's mother had said. Yes; and The Man needed to make it. There was a sort of categorical imperative involved—only I knew those were not the right words, for this experience had nothing to do with Kantian ethics or logic or even reason. Yet there *was* an imperative—

"And that is where Lamar Dodd comes in. I have never met him. But I have met his paintings. Now I'll have to go back— there is no chronology in this experience:

"As the years went by, after Ellen and I were married, and my knowledge of the world expanded just a little, and I saw its beauty and grandeur and delicacy and complexity and awful brutality, its art, and luxury and gaiety, I began to go back again and again to the little shack where I was born. And to my mother. I'd see her toting slops to the hogs; going in the cold to the outhouse when she was too ill to be out of bed; bringing in a heavy load of wood to cook supper with. Toiling like an animal, and feeling like a woman. . . . The more I read, the more plays I went to, the more museums I visited, the more my awareness of human experience deepened, the worse it got.

"A friend who had read a book of Freud's, or maybe a half chapter, said something to me about guilt in my relationship with her. Good God! I didn't have to feel guilt to be aware of what my mother had missed, of a life emptied of soft warm meanings. I have a profound respect for Freud. I don't have a bit for the fools who throw him in your face whenever they see you in pain. I simply could not accept my mother's toil-worn, animal life. I did not blame God, or Capitalism, or the South or the North, or Colonialism, or my father or any other devil for it—I had enough sense to know that a thousand years of human error had made my mother's life what it was. I wanted only to be at peace with my memory of her. That was all.

"One day—by this time, I was principal of a school and Ellen and I had been married many years and had two sons—I went over to the University of Georgia on business. After I had finished my chores, I looked for the art department. I had thought, suddenly, impulsively, I would like to look at a few paintings today. And so, I went over. And there I saw Lamar Dodd's work. I looked at those colors: the clay with sun on it, the clay with night deep inside it, the clay with the terror—the old red-purple clay on which I had slipped a thousand times; all the treachery of it was in that painting, the stickiness, the poverty, the bleakness and the ordeal. And yet it was singing at the top of its voice." Man, singing down his terror: standing off and looking at his ordeal, picking it up in his mind and heart and his hands, and making it smaller than himself; and sometimes, turning it into a thing so beautiful and true and precious that for a thousand years after he is dead, other men will care for it.

"I stood there looking, and crying as I looked. From relief. All my insides, everything in my life, sort of trembled and moved and rearranged itself as that painting reached down and lifted the pain off my childhood. I think, forever."

He smiled. "I have cried, I reckon, a half-dozen times since I was ten years old. I've told you of two of those times, tonight."

*Something in them needed that little applewood table.* He understood now. "I knew, too, how I had needed those paintings. I had been groping so long, trying to get it with my mind: my childhood and my parents' life. Just as I had tried to understand music and art with my mind. Of course you can't. Any more than I could understand Ellen that way. Or God. You've got to need art; when you need its voice, it speaks to you."

The little worm of a dream, the forgotten experience, metamorphosing into something strange and shimmering and eternal. And how that memory, that dream, can destroy you just as things can, if it doesn't free itself and get outside you.

Isn't it a strange, a wondrous thing: man's need of art! I don't pretend to understand it. I only know what it feels like.

So easy to understand the need for food, warmth, shelter, and the need we call sex. All animals share these. So easy to see also, because it is completely reasonable to anyone who has ever loved a child, the human need of tenderness and esteem; and Miss Molly's knowledge—man is at home with that part of his mind. All this, we know the necessity of; we are aware that man would never have left the animal kingdom nor would he be alive today had not these needs been met in some fashion.

But art—It is like one's need of God, I thought. Hard to justify it with words. (I know theologians and estheticians try, but we are worse off from their jargon, I think, sometimes.) But it seems to me that without art and without God a man can never come to terms with his past nor relate himself to his future. It is by means of the community of the dream that men share each other's deepest experiences. It is not natural to the animal kingdom; nor to the earth and the universe: this turning of a secret dream into something that has never existed before. But it is natural to men. And other men can look at it, touch it, or hear it and whisper Yes; I dreamed it too, only— only I could not put it together, and you, the artist, have done so.

And it is because men have dreamed of God and fallen in love with that dream that they can share their hopes and plans for a human future which they will never experience but which they believe in so deeply that they gladly give their lives for it.

Cephas . . . and his Susie.

"It is easy to see the little aborted artist in Susie—torn from the placenta of human resources and still trying to grow," I said aloud. "There it is; just barely alive, nourishing itself on the tree and on Revelations. But it is difficult to find the artist in Cephas—"

"Because his hate stirs up dust in our minds," Timothy said. "But don't you see, he, too, is trying to make that old privy-corncob past sing. When he was a little fellow he probably sat out there looking at pictures of things, things, things in a Sears, Roebuck catalog. Lord, Lord! *Everything modrun.* . . . To me, that is a fine line of poetry. It's got so much clay on it. God bless him. Oh, I know: he may blow us all to kingdom come. He jolly well may, you know, for the Cephases are the dictators' and the demagogues' right-hand men—and just the kind to want to drop bombs on folks, to hear the noise, or to stop the noise inside them."

## ~§ 11 §~

THE NEXT morning, I turned my car back toward the mountains. And all day, as the road led from swamp to rolling plains to hills, to mountains, I drove past small glass-walled air-conditioned landscaped factories that are popping up in the smallest towns; and past new rural hospitals and health centers; and fields that are contour-plowed and green with cover crops, and herds of fine cattle, and painted barns, and new chicken farms where Plymouth Rocks and White Leghorns and Barred Rocks crisscross the grass with the colors of an old-fashioned quilt—a sight as neat and sensibly patterned as a Grandma Moses painting and as new to us as is the idea of a sturdy lady in her eighties taking up painting and becoming world-famous for her refusal to succumb to the dullness and decay of old age.

Change. Quick change that came without bloodshed or dictator or the duress of secret police. But not without opposition. No. For we live in a democracy and people are free to speak out even against a good future for themselves—and often do. There were violent words and a frantic seeking for scapegoats during that change. There still are—even from those who have profited most by it: like Cephas. Cephas still thinks "the communists" had something to do with the change; not with *his* prosperity, of course, for Cephas thinks of himself as a "self-made man"; but with *change*. He fears the word with an intensity threatening all that is reasonable and brave in him. It gets too close, somehow, to his little private security system which he does not know how to change and as yet feels no need for changing. His way of finding "enemies" on which to blame his difficulties, his way of striking out verbally against them, his way of cutting loose from his past, has worked very well for his physical and economic health—so far. (That it may be dangerous for the rest of us, and his grandchildren, has never occurred to him.) But he does not feel good inside; there is not much peace within soul and mind; and so, he builds himself fine new defenses to pile on top of the old ones which served him well as a child. Piling up *things* to make higher his antique fort. . . .

Somehow, because of experiences and lack of experiences in childhood which I know nothing about—in the home? at school? down the lane?—Cephas has related himself to *things* without relating himself to the human beings who made them, who use them, who dreamed them up. And because he cannot relate them to their creators and their users, *things* have taken on a powerful dehumanized life of their own in his mind. They have become, in a twisted odd way, as ghosty and hypnotic as are Susie's tree children. For Cephas is human even though the things are not, and he has—he is compelled to have—a relationship with them. (If not a rational one—then, inevitably, a symbolic one.) And now—it seemed to me—the things have *him* in their clutch. *Everything modrun* is the new mark of peonage on Cephas's life. On his, only? No, on mine too; and my fellow countrymen's. We have not yet got on top of the new experience of machine-made abundance, we have not mastered the ordeal of prosperity—not because we have "too much," but because we forget about the applewood table. We have not yet learned to make a great painting out of the old eroded past. We find it so hard to teach our new machine-made terrors to sing. We try—every one of us tries—and yet the harmonic resolution of this exciting modern progression of dissonance on dissonance on dissonance still eludes us.

Timothy and Ellen? They had found a better way. They told me so much about themselves, that night, with laughter and something close to tears, now and then. Recollecting in tranquility—or as close to it as one can get when communicating with others. For in the act of real communication a hollow needle is often plunged deep into the memory, drawing out through the dispassionately (or lightly) told event a stream of feelings that often stain the tranquil moment with archaic hurts.

Three weeks after they were married Tim and Ellen began to teach a two-room school out in the country.

"We taught and we learned; we went to Columbia University's Teachers College to get our Master's degree as a lot of country teachers do. Our trips to New York were pilgrimages to listen to great music, to look at great skyscrapers, and great paintings and great sculpture in the Metropolitan and the Museum of Modern Art and the other museums whose names we hardly knew. The word in our minds was *great*. We may have stared and craned our necks too much but we felt reverence. It was Mecca. We drank from the Pierian springs. We looked upon Olympus. New York is like that, even now, to a lot of Americans. And then we'd relax and go to an East Side restaurant for one elegant and much too expensive dinner and to the theatre and afterward we'd walk up and down Times Square, loving the lights and the bold bright phoniness. And always we'd go to Chinatown. And after we'd eaten at Lee's we'd walk under the El to the Bowery and look at that wasteland and quote Stephen Crane to each other. And always we ended our pilgrimage by making the circle tour around Manhattan in a boat.

"One summer we went to Europe. It was almost spoiled for me because Miss Molly was not with us. If she had only been there . . . she would have pulled time back and forth like she used to and we'd have talked with Erasmus and Descartes and Locke. And we'd have gone to da Vinci's workshop at Milan, and with hearts beating out of us, maybe we could have felt the great dream and the great fact struggling for possession of a genius's soul. And there would have been time for a little chat with Napoleon on his lonely island—can't you see Miss Molly there? And Lord God, how she would have made us tremble at the sight of Machiavelli! We would have walked along the Avon and asked Shakespeare if he was really Shakespeare and he would have told Miss Molly the truth; Daumier would have taken us to courtrooms and sketched those wonderful old scoundrels for us, and maybe Hugo might have met us in the nave of Notre Dame—no, under a gargoyle, for Miss Molly would have liked it that way—and perhaps he would have told us more about those deep meanings which he never quite wrote down in his books. (Or was it I who missed the meanings in my greed for what-happened-next?) And she would have taken us to walk among the broken columns of Greece—in moonlight, too—in company with Sophocles, and smiled with Aristophanes at the cartoon strip which man, too often, makes of his great destiny. And we might have felt our roots pushing deep into that past, if only Miss Molly had been there. . . . But it was pretty good, anyway."

"I was glad she did not see the rest of it," said Ellen, in her quiet even voice.

For it was the summer of 1938. Integrity had been liquidated in Moscow and minds and bodies were being liquidated all over Germany. They saw Hitler and those twisted men surrounding him march in to the magnificent music of a distinguished German orchestra playing a Beethoven symphony. They heard him speak, and felt the deep and awful emotions surging and pounding in that crowd.

The great monster was on the prowl. Intent now on befouling all that the creative spirit of man has dreamed and brought forth. Wherever they went, they felt it: not only in the Reichstag; its shadow was everywhere that summer. In the Louvre, in bistros and sidewalk cafés, in the churches of Florence, in Geneva, Stockholm, London—

"It was at home, too; but we had not realized it until we got to Europe."

You'd see it in men's faces; hear it in their words, feel it in the gesture of bodies. In Russia a great and good dream had died because men had separated it from human values. The stench of that corpse was drifting across Europe and the world.

"Maybe it was stillborn. Yes," Timothy said slowly, "it never really lived for it was not about human beings at all. It was about *things*. You'd think something dead couldn't hurt folks.

But hungry men feed on dreams that have died—that is, if the undertaker does a good job of fixing them up pretty."

Someone opened the door of the office. Timothy went in to see what was needed. And while he was gone, Ellen told me about their two sons: young Tim in Atlanta, and Henry in Korea. Tim had gone to Georgia Tech, and was now in an architect's office. Henry had had a year at Chapel Hill before going into military service. As she talked, I began to feel Ellen's quality. It was so quiet. No prettiness in it. No edges to it. No fireworks as in Tim. Something deeply accepting of life, maternal and durable as hemp. I thought of that great artist, Kaethe Kollwitz, whose drawings and etchings *are* the maternal spirit. Children . . . food . . . life—Ellen felt responsible for. There was no Madonna-and-Child glow on Ellen. I looked at her strong stubby fingers. Fine warm eyes. Robust body. Felt again her strength and goodness.

Timothy was back now. Ellen made a pot of coffee, brought in a plate of sandwiches. It was then that they told me about the two women.

"As stormy as tonight," said Timothy. "And as late." A car drove up. Parked. Lights on. No one came in. Timothy waited ten minutes, then put on his slicker and went out. In the car were two Negro women. Well dressed, and terribly scared. "I asked them if I could help them. One said (and I never heard a more beautiful speaking voice), 'We do not know what to do next. The storm—it is late—and we know no place to go. Could you, would you suggest a Negro family who might possibly take us in? If you will be so kind—'

"I got sick at my stomach. Here was a place supposed to be open to strangers. And this was America; my country; theirs, too; and I loved it and was proud of it and had good cause to be proud of it, and they have good cause too. Yet, *this* question could be asked.

"I said—and God help me, do you know I was more scared than when I got the shrapnel in my hip at Argonne!—I said, If you would care to stay here, there is a vacant room and I believe you would be comfortable.

"One stared at me as if I had accosted her. The other never looked up. I don't know what they were thinking—a white man had—I just don't know what came into their minds. But there was no trust in their faces. So I called my wife. Ellen came out in the rain and invited them in. We put them in room seven. We both went with them and got them settled. They paid the fee and filled out a card. And I heard Ellen say as quietly as her mother would have spoken, 'If you ladies would like breakfast, we begin to serve at seven o'clock.' I almost yelled *Ellen, what in the name of God are you saying! This is Geor*—And then, inside me suddenly, I knelt down.

"Yeah. I asked Him to forgive me for my sin. I saw it as plain as Saul of Tarsus saw his on the road to Damascus. I had done what was right to do but with only half of me. And Ellen had done what was right with her whole heart."

"Because of Henry's letter, Tim," she said softly.

"You remembered. I half-remembered. Well anyway, they said No, they'd leave early. About six o'clock."

So Timothy and Ellen went to their rooms back of the office. Ellen sat at her dressing table, brushing her hair. She would stop brushing, place the hairpins in two rows, mix them up, rearrange them, brush her hair again. Then once more, arrange the hairpins. "I knew something was coming," said Timothy.

Each read for a while as they always did after the day's work was over, but the pages of her book were not turning. When he clicked off the light she said, "Tim . . . there comes a time in a life when if you don't go the second mile, you'll never take another step. You'll sit there the rest of your days justifying why you didn't move. That time has come for me." And he said, "O. K. Ellen. My muscles feel like a little hike might be the very thing to take the kinks out of them, too."

Next morning at five-thirty they took a breakfast tray to room seven. "There was nowhere, and we knew it, for them to get a cup of coffee."

Young Henry's letter had arrived only a few weeks before. He had been wounded in the leg on Christmas Hill. Got lost from his outfit, made his way through the dark toward the rear, never knowing where he was or at what moment a Chinese or North Korean gun would stop him. He had stumbled against something hard. An American voice spoke softly. He answered. A hand pulled him in to shelter. And he blacked out. When he came to, he felt a bandage on his leg. The voice told him the enemy was close. Better not talk. Struck a light to see about you, the voice said, but better not, no more. How close? Couldn't tell. But loneliness made them whisper now and then, each telling the other where he was from. Georgia. Alabama. Each telling how long he had been out. One year. Two years. Then they went to sleep. When Henry woke up at dawn, he felt something on his chest. Saw a black hand resting there. "And I lay, Mother, and looked at it. And you know all I was thinking for you and Dad have thought it too. He'd risked that light to tend to me and he saw I was white when he did it. I just lay there, thinking. By the time he woke up, I'd been home and back, through my whole life and back. And I knew something. I knew when I went home, I was going to have Bud come visit me. And if I haven't got the guts to do it —because I know you and Dad have—then I hope a bullet will get me. I'd deserve a communist prison but I'd settle for a little less."

"We were sort of getting ready for Bud's visit," Timothy chuckled. "Honey," he shook the coffee pot, "is there a bit of something left in the refrigerator?" While he was foraging, Ellen told more about the motor court. Timothy had been advised by the doctors to keep off his feet. The hip had been giving him trouble. He was not the sitting-down kind of teacher so they took their savings and began a new life. "It seemed the next best thing to teaching," she said. "A motor court out in the country has a special meaning for Tim. It is, for him, a symbol of something new and exciting that is happening in the world."

"Yes," he said, putting down glasses of milk and a plate of peaches. "There *is* something wonderful happening. But we say so much about the dangers that we have not yet looked at what is being born."

To him, the most significant event of our age is not atomic power but the new power of a billion and a half rural people of Asia and Africa, waking up: "moving, learning, participating, making decisions.

"For ten thousand years, country folks have been on the banks of the river gawking at the city guys in there running boats up and down, building dams, stealing from each other and all the rest of it. But they're in the river now. And it's swollen and in flood, and dangerous as the devil, of course. But they're there and they'll be there from here on out. And no political system, no group of clever politicians, can dam up that energy for long. I know the communists are trying but they can no more control a billion and a half rural people who have suddenly heard they're important, than their secret police could scare a Mississippi flood."

Timothy was walking up and down as he talked. "It means a lot to me: the country folks waking up everywhere and feeling human and important. For the first time in recorded history. Think of it! Maybe I'm identifying with them too much. But what is happening is dramatic and earth-shaking and we do not yet realize the tremendous story in it. The terrific power that is being released, suddenly, in the world . . . the strong, sure feeling for life that they will bring to human affairs. . . .

"What they know about *is* life. They know you raise a crop with work and manure and by begging God for a little rain, and a lot of sun, and then just squatting there and watching it grow, and hoping, and never giving up. Birth and death, and growing things—these are as familiar as sunrise and dark. But logic? Abstractions? No.

"Rural folks may be dumb as an ox about some things but they have a sense of continuity. Earthiness. Humor. Canniness.

"For instance: any countryman knows if you pull up a stalk of corn to see what it is like, you are looking not at corn growing but corn dying. And there's a heck of a difference. But a lot of bright folks in laboratories don't know that, yet. Isn't this one of the big troubles today: we don't always know when the corn is growing and when it is dying. And because we don't remember what rural folks take for granted, even the scientists get all mixed up. That is why many sensible people fear "science": psychology, psychiatry, sociology, even medical science; and now, once more, they are fearing the physical sciences. They've got a resistance. And some of it comes from asinine reasons. But some of it makes good sense. Because they've lost faith in science's validity for man. Why? Because they know in their bones that you can't take a piece of a man and look at it, whether it's his childhood or his liver or his mind and see it as it really is, if it is separated from the whole organism and the man's whole life. They can't tell you why, but they know it, just as their old grannies knew things in *their* bones. And they know, too, that the physical scientists devalued man when they tried to keep moral values out of their branch of science—and ended up with the bomb now threatening all human life. The ordinary folks see that abstracting may be the way man acquires knowledge but it is a quick sure way for him to destroy himself, too. Unless he uses that knowledge *for men*.

"And the same basic falseness is in every political system, to-day. For instance: take a belief, a sweet and warm and beautiful belief like the importance of the human being and the importance of giving him enough freedom and helping him find enough responsibility to keep growing as a human being (the belief our religion is based on and all real religions are based on); and then separate that belief from life and values, from integrity and honor, and tie it up with things and with the way folks happen to be making their money at the moment, and then let a bunch of greedy men armed with atomic weapons begin to manipulate all that together to get power for themselves—and well, you've got a hell of a mess, believe me. And this is what is happening in every political system across the face of the earth, today. Every system, the best and the worst, wants to *use* men and their deep needs and their tenderest beliefs to build power for a political party.

"Don't get me wrong. I believe in government. Government of human beings by human beings for human goals. And in my way of thinking, that means something free and flexible. And the word *democracy* is still good enough to describe it, for me. But the people in every country have got to put the politician in his place. He needs to be told that he has no divine rights, and there is nothing divine about his political party, either. He seems to feel that, like the old kings and feudal lords, he is exempt from moral standards and is above such plain homespun qualities as good will and integrity, and that his 'party' is more important than the people. I have so deep a reverence for the artist and the poet, the scientist (when he is humble) and the prophet—and yes, the statesman, the selfless statesman: because they create. They bind us together. They keep us tied to time. But you could dump all the politicians on a boat and sink it and what would happen? Nothing. Except, maybe, folks could have one long sweet night of sleep. But if you dumped the world's art, its knowledge—ah, then. . . .

"Now that makes me feel better," Timothy said and laughed heartily. "Even though I know I don't really mean it. We all have a few favorites that we'd like to keep off that boat."

He pulled at his red hair. Grinned. "Now where was I? Anyway, the rural people of the world are not going to move according to anybody's pet system. Not even America's. (That's it. Now I'm back on the track.) They are not going in for ideologies. They'll keep watching to see if the stalk of corn is still in the ground, growing. At least, I hope to God they will.

Their natural cunning and shrewdness and humor may slow down this ideology madness. It can. If only—

"If only they think of themselves as persons more important than things, more important than any government, more important than any way of making money, or any ideology, if they believe that, understand it the way they understand things growing in their fields, they can control this tremendous energy of theirs and bring themselves in an orderly, creative way into what we call civilization. And they'll give it the biggest shot in the arm it's had in a thousand years.

"That is, if people who really care, help them. They must have the good teacher. Not the inquisitor. If they only had Miss Molly!" He laughed. "I mean that. For the great problem today is how to get that belief to them quickly enough. The communist trick is to feed them a little bread, a little belief, a little hope and then load them down with fear. It won't work. Not for long. Maybe with a few. But not for long.

"Funny thing . . . a man will let his fears kill him; and he is easily persuaded to die for them; but he digs in and lives because of something he believes in. And it's got to concern his soul and body and child and it's got to be bigger than all of them.

"But how you going to do it? How can you get a billion and a half people to believe they are important because they have a significant role to play in God's—not a dictator's—universe? And do it while you're keeping the exploiters away from them? It is a man-size job, all right. And the most important one of our time.

"When you think of their poverty. . . ." Timothy came back

to that theme again and again, that night. "My dad's old share-cropping cabin? It was a mansion compared to what some of the people of India and China and Indonesia and Iran and Rhodesia live in. They need houses. They need bread. They need to learn to read and write. But giving them a roof, a loaf of bread, and a book won't turn them from 'the masses' into the people. They've got to have esteem. And a love of knowledge. And a belief in human destiny.

"And so," he stopped, looked at his two listeners, took a drink of milk. Laughed. "Reckon I'd better slide out of the stratosphere. Anyway, one day, Ellen and I built us a motor court on a paved highway. Sound's about as anticlimactic as you could imagine. But it isn't. Since we can no longer live and work with children, we want to live the rest of our lives close to the stranger: as his friends. To do our share of getting the world connected up. The old days of distance and darkness are about over in America. We rural folks are getting connected up fast with the rest of the world. And I'd like to think it soon will be happening everywhere.

"It is just one small dream," he said quietly. "Ellen's and mine. And in a way it doesn't amount to two cents. But a million small dreams. . . . It is really the only way to work the mess out. For each of us, wherever we are, out in the country, at a filling station, in town in the bank or store, in school, or library, to keep tying ourselves, in friendliness, to children and to the stranger. Keeping ourselves plugged in to time and space. If we don't do it in our individual way, then some smart politician is going to convince us it is easier 'just to leave it to him' to settle the world's problems."

And then they told me how their new life had worked out. The first month they opened the court, a Pakistani came in to spend the night. "We were as thrilled as two kids," Ellen said. "We felt we were really in touch with the world. He was a country boy, too. Used camels on his farm. But they have a tractor now. He gave me his mother's recipe for rice pilaf—or as near it as he could remember. And when he went to his room he took Thomas Wolfe's *Look Homeward, Angel* and Mumford's *The Condition of Man* to read." One time, a Chinese from Hangchow came. "A very learned man who told us of Mo Ti, a great Chinese philosopher of whom we had never heard. He had read Thoreau in Mission School and took our copy to reread. And once, two Indians came who had met Gandhi. We had a beautiful evening of talk," said Timothy. Not long ago a Turk spent two days; he didn't hesitate when he looked at the books: pulled out Sandburg's *Lincoln*, all six volumes, and took them to bed with him. "I think he stayed two days because he could not bear to stop reading them." And there was an old couple from Idaho, rather poorly dressed, Timothy said, "who looked as if they came out of the kind of little burg that used to fire up Sinclair Lewis. They talked all evening, in the most learned fashion, too, about Goethe. Had Ellen and me reading *Faust* and *Wilhelm Meister* again."

One night, a girl came in to use the phone. It was near Christmas. Tim and Ellen had been trimming the tree and hanging the prints of Italian Primitives which they put on the walls at that time. Tim had been chanting Byron Reece's

> *If I but had a little coat,*
> *A coat to fit a no-year-old,*

*I'd button it close about His throat*
*To cover Him from the cold,*
*The cold,*
. *To cover Him from the cold....*

Working, and talking about Christmas, about their two boys.
They did not go into the office. Saw her, heard her voice at the
phone, heard the door open and shut. A few minutes later, Tim
went in for a ball of twine, called, "We got a Christmas present." There was a baby in a basket near the phone. A little girl.
Tim had never had a sister or a daughter. "Maybe it *is* a present," he kept saying. His wife said now, "I think he believed it
for just a moment. He couldn't take his eyes off of it." An hour
later, the girl was back. Ellen was holding the sleeping baby.
Tim was looking at it. "Oh, thank you, thank you," she said
breathlessly, softly, took it gently out of Ellen's arms, laid it in
the basket, picked up the basket and was gone.

"Now what *that* adds up to, I just don't know. Or what it all
adds up to? I'm not sure. Perhaps only something good and
interesting for Ellen and me. That may be all."

And then Ellen reminded us that it was very late and we told
each other good-by.

I liked their dream. "For the first time in history, rural folks
will be the world's host," he had said. The day of the grand old
hotels like Shepheard's in Cairo is over. They belonged to a
Colonial dream as dead as I hope Hitler's is and Stalin's soon
will be. After all, the three had a lot to do with each other and
should die together. "Soon these little roadside inns will be
everywhere: in Ceylon, the villages of India, out in Szechwan,
in the desert. Even in Russia, maybe. Wherever there is a high-

way or landing strip, you'll find them. Right out in the sticks."

I hope he is right. And that they will have hosts and hostesses as kind and friendly and generous and as interesting as Timothy and Ellen. Welcoming all strangers. Giving and receiving gifts of the mind and spirit. Host and guest sharing old childhood memories with each other—and their mothers' recipes, and their concern and ideas for a more harmonious world. Women talking about their babies and their homes; men talking about the crops and business; and now and then, perhaps a few men and women will talk quietly together about poetry. What political ideology can equal such simple communication as a means of bringing us closer together? We won't have to hunt a common ground: we will have found it in our children and homes and everyday affairs, and in our art and our memories and dreams. We will have entered, then, the great age of communication about meaningful things: an age when the power of man's inner resources, so long walled off by anxiety, will at last be available to him.

I was dreaming, too, now. Timothy was the kind of man who made good dreams seem possible. And Ellen made them seem so sensible.

*Then burn em. Burn em all up. . . . Tell you what I think: I think every Communist and Catholic ought to be run out of the country, and there's nobody but Joe who's got the guts to do it. And while he's doing it, he can take the Jews, too.* Down the road a piece from Timothy's, lived Cephas. In a fine modern motor court. Both had come from sharecroppers' cabins. Both had traveled the same old clay-sand road. What made the difference?

Was it because of the adventitious entrance and departure of

certain people in their lives? Timothy had his Good Teacher.
And Cephas did not have her. But how do I know? There must
have been in Miss Molly's schoolroom a few little boys like
Cephas, too. They were not all Timothys in those homemade
desks. Not all of her pupils went with her on those treks across
the world and back into our past. No. Some of them must have
stayed right there in the drab schoolroom, like little vegetables;
and others, even if they tagged along, must have been thinking
not about truth and tenderness and the wonder of being alive
and the miracle of the imagination and the pleasure of being
aware that one is aware, but about *things*, already on the hunt
for them; and some, like Susie, were not thinking at all but
dreaming of creatures who have never been born playing in
petrified primeval forests distant and quiet as the moon.

Whatever made the difference in them must have begun
earlier than when a Miss Molly walked or failed to walk into
their lives. The nudging and pushing and turning that sends
one of us in this direction and one in that must have begun long
before we opened our First Reader. Tenderness or lack of it in
the home? Someone there, or not there, who loved knowledge
even though possessing little of it? Someone there, or not there,
who esteemed himself as a person and felt linked, somehow, to
human destiny? It may be. Differences of innate intelligence?
Bodies different in glandular and muscular quality? Metabolic
differences? It may be all of these. We know so little, as yet,
about how Timothy comes out of one shack and Cephas out of
another and what makes an Ellen from a fine big house care
more for people than things, and what ties Susie to a fantasy
world made of immortal children and mortal time, and lets her
out only to do a good little Samaritan deed each Sunday.

We know so little. But we are beginning to realize that it is not thing-poverty and fact-ignorance alone that make the difference. For you can match these men in their creative and lamentable qualities, in their private security systems and their psychic resources and deprivations, on the richest avenues of the world. You will find Timothys and Cephases in the yards of Harvard and Yale and Oxford, down on Wall Street, in bishoprics; as surgeons in great hospitals, as scientists in famed laboratories, as publishers and as authors; you find them when they are young as easily at Groton as in a one-room school. And Susie and Ellen? They are often each other's sisters. Brush off the top layer of manners, clothes and speech—and there they are.

No, I thought as I drove along that day, it is not money and facts that make the real differences. It is something closer to one's body and the people one loves (or fails to love) and as distant as God that drives one man to bind himself to his human world and another to keep slashing at his ties.

## 12

I ASKED her the question for I had known her since she was a child.

She said, "I didn't find my way. Not for a long time. If John had been here—but he was in Korea. His letters—I couldn't have done without them—and there was Bill's surgeon, a wonderful man—and friends. All of it helped. But I was lost. And I failed Bill.

"It's the suddenness of it. He was skating with the neighborhood children. I called to him as he left the house to be careful, something might happen. I never believed it would. You don't. You just say it. When the telephone rang I was washing my hair. I let it ring until I had rinsed the soap out, thinking it was one of the girls. Then I ran downstairs to answer it.

"Sometimes, even now, it wakes me in the night—the ringing."

I was visiting in Marty's home for a few days. And as we talked, we were on our way to the school to pick up Bill. She did not say more until traffic cleared.

"I had nothing inside me to meet it," she said. "I had always believed it could never happen to me. And when it did, there was nothing there—not even a little mental first-aid kit."

The boys were racing. A truck swerved around the corner. No one was hurt but Bill. His arms were so injured that they had to be amputated close to the shoulders. For a few days the doctors were not certain that Bill could make it. There had been a severe concussion, much loss of blood, a long wait for an ambulance. But finally things leveled off and he was out of danger.

"When I knew what the score was, I—it will shock you. Bill's surgeon told me it was natural—at least, other people do it, sometimes—and I've tried to believe him. I—left Bill. I went to the hospital every day, my body did; but deep down in me I wasn't there. I had gone to look—"

She told me how she searched her life through, looking . . . for two little lost arms. Asking herself why it had happened, what had she done or failed to do, dragging out memories, turning them over, raveling them out to find an answer. As if, once an answer were found, then somehow, in a magic way, those arms would be restored.

She had spoken to him at breakfast that morning about his table manners. And then, as he dashed off to skate with the other children she had called to him to be careful. "I began to think—crazy things." If she had not told him to be careful, maybe it wouldn't have happened. Maybe she had nagged him too much. Maybe he had to show her he could be reckless to keep her from ruining him. The sensible part of her, the sane part, told her she was not a nagger. *But why did I tell him something might happen! Did I know it was going to happen— did I want it to happen—was that why I warned him?* The sane part told her that though skating is a reasonable risk for children to take, and Bill was alert and careful, it was right, even so, for her to warn him of danger.

"But they were like somebody else's words. Not mine."

And then she began to go back to that breakfast, raking over its small events. It was as if the room had frozen. A streak of sun across the table—a spot of jam on the checked cloth—Bill's yellow cereal bowl—the clock ticking. Nothing changed in that still life for months. "I went back a thousand times to find what I had done, or failed to do," she said. "As if I had to touch every small part of that morning again and again."

Bill had gulped his cereal, and she had scolded him. Then Bill tilted his bowl and slurped the milk. She thought, If he does it again, I'll— She spoke sharply. And he stared at her—even the little cowlick brushed back slick and wet stared at her as if both believed her their mortal enemy. And then he said in a low voice, "I wish Daddy would come home. I do wish it! I wish it, I wish it!" And she wished it, too, for she was dead tired of being mama and papa both, but it had hurt to hear him say it.

After he left to go skating, she felt that she could not go on alone, another minute, without John.

"I was breaking up like the pieces of a puzzle and knew I'd better do something quick. So I washed my hair. When the phone rang, I didn't answer at once because—well, I didn't feel very gay and my friends always expect me to be on top of the world. As I say this to you, it could be something I read somewhere. It still doesn't feel as if it happened to me. . . ."

Her questions kept on. And always she felt she must answer them.

"I'd be in the kitchen cooking, forgetting for a moment—and it would start. I felt compelled to answer—as if Teacher were there, or something—a presence—I don't know—that would not leave me alone. Was I a morbid kid? Too guilty about things? I don't remember that I worried much." She glanced at me quickly. "Or maybe I did and forgot it. I don't know. But they kept on, the questions."

"No one can answer them. Of course we should never try."

"Well, I tried. And it went on and on, for a long time. Like a dream in which you are caught. You try to wake up. You can't."

I know. Perhaps we all know that dream in which everything changes its name and its face and all the signs are up in the wrong places and you can't find home, anywhere.

"And Bill's surgeon, bless him, just kept talking to me," she said, after a few minutes. "He is the kind of surgeon who doesn't leave you after an operation. He stood by, operating on Bill's life until he was sure it was worth living again." And as he worked with Bill and fitted his new arms, he kept operating on Marty, too, telling her in his calm, sure voice how the human body restores its functions if only the mind and heart will help it a little, building a picture of human strength, trying to cut away her fear.

"It is a strange thing," she said slowly, "how you hold on to fear. I didn't want it amputated—even though it was poisoning me. But he kept talking, so calmly and quietly."

He explained to her the process of making small canals through the muscles of chest and shoulder—cineplastic canals, he called them—and fastening the new arms to the pegs inserted in these canals, so that the muscles—the pectoral and

others—can control the arm's movements. And he took her to
see people who were using their new arms, all the while quietly
reminding her that Bill, some day, would control his as skill-
fully. "He will be able to do miraculous things," he told her.
And he told her more: how the brain has many resources for a
hurt body to fall back on. Emergency reserves that most of us
never need and never use. But they are there, waiting: nerves,
ready to set up a new system of communication, of movement;
ready to go to work when we say the word. "And it meant
nothing to me," she said. "I heard the words but they had no
meaning."

As the physical therapist exercised Bill, he talked to her, too,
telling her what a fine strong son she had, how the muscles in
chest and torso had grown hard, what a beautiful balance he
had acquired, and so quickly. "Losing your arms does tricks to
your balance, much as the loss of wings does to a plane." Bill
was determined to play ball again and worked long hours on
his exercises—

"And instead of feeling proud, I didn't feel at all. It was as if
things were on two levels: on one I could see and hear, I knew
what was going on but I couldn't feel it; on the other I was
feeling but I didn't know what was happening.

"I got up one morning with the same nagging pain between
my shoulders that had been there since the accident, and ran
downstairs to make a cup of coffee. While the coffee was drip-
ping, I went to the window. The trees were bare. I don't think
I even looked at first. Then I saw that the buds had begun to
swell, and it was raining—a slow soft rain like we used to have
at home in the hills. I stood there, leaning against the cold
windowpane, remembering how Mother would let us make

candy on rainy days, and how I'd run out to see about my calf. I'd bring the little wet thing inside the barn if it had strayed out, and it was always warm and good in there. . . . And I remembered suddenly a crocheted throw—made of purple and yellow and black and red squares, not very pretty but I loved it —which Mother would wrap around me when I was sick—

"And then it happened. Somehow I was looking in a different direction and I saw—everything. How do you explain it? I can't. It was as if I had awakened from a deep and terrible sleep. Maybe that is what I did. I knew where I was. I was *here* and Bill was *here,* I could touch him."

And she began to feel for the first time, that morning, what Bill was going through. This was *his* ordeal that she was engaged in, not hers. It was as if she were inside him, feeling what he felt, looking at what he saw ahead of him. "I felt the distance"—how far away everything seems to you if you have no arms to touch it. And the little things—what it was like to want to pick up your knife or turn the radio dial, or run a comb through your hair.

"I realized all he would miss, all of it." She had known it, yes; but she had not felt it or understood its meaning, until that moment. Her feelings had gathered around herself, walling her off from Bill. Now, once more, she was connected.

"I felt him," she said again and again. And slowly it came to her: it didn't matter what she had done or failed to do; only one thing mattered now and that was Bill; Bill, this minute, and the life he was going to live.

"So I came home." She smiled and parked the car across the street from Bill's school. "I still don't know where I had been."

We waited for the children to come out of school and neither of us talked for a while. Then she said, "He knew." And she told me. She had gone to the hospital and as usual, Bill was staring out of the window. He slowly turned when he heard her. And quickly his eyes reached out and caught her and held on as if they'd never let go, just as he used to do when he was little and she had been away all day.

That was the hard moment. "When I saw how completely I had failed him I almost forgot him the second time, worrying over that." She smiled quickly to push back the tears. "It's like flypaper—once you get on it."

Bill came running across the school yard with his books and his kite and his little friend, Jenny.

"She was with him when it happened," Marty said.

They stopped, searched the cars, found us, dashed across the street. It was spring and a fine, soft day and we were going on a picnic down by the river.

The two of them climbed into the back seat, Bill checked to see if his fishing tackle was there, we turned into the river road.

After lunch, the youngsters went off to dig bait. Marty picked up a book, settled down under a tree. And I sat under another tree, not reading but thinking of her, of those questions which had kidnaped her—and Bill too—and left them on a lost road; thinking of that little memory which, like a firm, loving hand, had brought her back to her real world again. Rain . . . a limb of a tree . . . buds swelling . . . the cool windowpane against her cheek . . . and suddenly she had access, once more, to the love within her nature. All because a memory had the mysterious power, somehow, to set off chain reactions of memories, of beliefs, until at last the way cleared to the creative, fusing, loving part of her and she found the strength to accept her future—and Bill's.

Beyond us, I could hear Bill and Jenny calling to each other, counting the worms, dashing from one place to a better.

As I looked up, Marty laid her book aside and told me about the two:

Jenny lived next door. She was a shy, withdrawn little thing when they first knew her, who found it difficult to do the things other children do easily. So Bill took over as teacher. He would put her up in front on his bike when he was eight and she was six and take her around with him. He taught her to ride her bicycle when it was given her that Christmas. He taught her to skate and swim and to ride his pony. It was Jenny who gave the policeman Marty's telephone number. And Jenny who gave him quickly and clearly the other information he needed. But when her mother told her about Bill's arms, she did not say a word. She got up and went to her room and began to read a book. She did not mention it when she was with her parents. Days passed and she did not ask to see Bill. It was as if she had wrapped herself up and laid "the package" away where all that had happened could never touch her again. But they knew that each of us has our way of fitting ourselves to the sharp edges of a disaster like this, and being wise parents, they did not press her.

One night, shortly afterward, a storm came up. Jenny's father went into her room to see about the windows. When he came out, he said, "I want you to go see Jenny."

They went in quietly and by his flashlight, they looked at

their child, asleep, covers half off, her arms tied down to her body with a heavy cord, from her shoulders to her wrists. She had to find out what it felt like.

At breakfast, they did not comment on the red lines on her arms. They told her they were going to see Bill and invited her to come along. "I have a friend," said Jenny's father, "who is a fine tennis player. It happens that he lost his right arm when he was young. But he can beat me any day on the courts."

Jenny did not ask one question but her father answered all of them that had been written on her face for days.

"My friend has a cineplastic arm," he said. "A hook is on it. He wears a hand when he wants to." He told her about cineplastic arms. About wearing a hook. About "cosmetic hands."

"It all depends on Bill's nerve, how he comes through this," he said. "And that of course depends a lot on Bill's friends."

After a little more talk, Marty returned to her book. And I sat there remembering her when she was ten, twelve, fifteen, for she had spent many summers as a camper on our mountain. Had I been asked to choose from among the children in my camp those for whom one could reasonably predict success in meeting a trouble as big as this, Marty's name would not have crossed my mind. The little black-haired girl with the big eyes who was scared of thunderstorms? So pale when she saw someone hurt? Who used to say, when we talked of books, "Has it a happy ending? If not, count me out"? When not frightened of life, she was busy playing tricks on it. And like the little clown she was, she never smiled at her own jokes. After the camp was asleep, one night, she hung all her cabin-mates' shoes and her own on the limbs of trees. The next morning, she slept late, apparently unaware of the excitement, came to breakfast with feet bound with Grecian thongs, her wonderful long black hair in a Psyche knot, and a volume of Emily Dickinson's poems in her hands. Everyone loved this child for her foolery; it was a façade that served her well, though it was of tissue-paper thinness and easily ripped to the anxiety beneath.

It was the custom, at this camp, for children and counselors to talk frankly about themselves and this world they live in. And there were, among them, many who understood as much about those feelings that bind us together or sometimes tear us apart as they did about tennis and swimming. They had traveled a little way, at least, into the two worlds we live in, and talked about it with humility and insight and humor. But not Marty. During these talks, she was evasive and restless. Or she would begin to giggle—so infectiously that all of us would join in her laughter and that would be the end of seriousness for that day.

Even in those years, there were traces of strength in her, character prints that a good sleuth might have looked for. Marty gave up quickly on a job but always went back and carried it through. On the tennis court, in the sculpture room, down would go the racquet, the clay. A walkout. Then her return, grimly determined, as if there were another little girl in her who could not fail. There were other fragments that I remembered: Marty and a sick kitten, a rejected dog, a limpy rabbit, or in her hand a dazed bird who had flown head-on into the glass wall of the dining room. And her heroes, heroines, her "crushes" as the campers called them, in books, out of books, to whom she had a stubborn, ardent faithfulness. Somehow, her ego's strengths and weaknesses found a precarious balance among these giants and pygmies which she collected or created out of her need and surrounded herself with.

It was her curious rhythm of failure-success that I thought of now. There was the day she was thrown from a horse. Rather badly shaken up. Cried for a long time. Next day, she was back at the stables, ready to ride, insisted on the same horse when the instructor suggested a more amiable nag, and saw it through successfully—white to the lips. This was the Marty underneath the mask so frivolously painted, underneath the easy fear and panic that often showed through.

I sat there, listening to the children's voices, to the *shush* of turning page as she read her book, thinking of what she had told me. Yes, she had run away—from her responsibility and a future she could not bear to face. She had "left Bill."

But it seemed to me that, this time, it was not so much a flight as a search. Something in her beyond words, primitive, irrational, but human and natural, had rushed out after those arms just as a mother would leave her other children to find the child who is lost. The rest of Bill was *there*. It could wait. What was lost had to be recovered. So that he could be whole again. So that she could be whole again. For Marty thought of herself not only as the reflection she saw in her mirror changing but seeming to remain always the same; not only as the girl loved by John, and her parents' child, but as the mother of Bill, too. On a shadowy wordless level, as deep as those somatic processes which keep one's heart beating and lungs breathing, he was an extension in time and space of her image of herself. And so she "left" him, in order to find the old image of herself *and* him— that could never exist again. What an ancient drama it is!

Human beings forever trying to make whole what is broken; so often destroying their future in a desperate effort to restore their past. It is so easy to call it "self-destructiveness." But I don't think it is. Marty was trying to create something. The trouble was, she worked with unreal materials. It was as if she were an artist trying to paint a portrait with fantasy tubes of color. The canvas, after all her effort, was still blank.

One day, she realized this. She began to see that she had tried to make with the materials of childish guilt what can be created only out of mature love. And she came back from the past in time to help Bill grow a real life for himself.

Jenny had caught a fish; she was squealing, she wanted help to get it off the line, and Bill was taking it off for her. . . .

"John—" Marty looked up from her book. "From the beginning, he was different from me. It was Bill that he thought of, not himself, not me. Bill's life." She could not get in touch with him at first; he had gone up to one of the islands on a mission. At last he heard and phoned her. "I shall remember his voice as long as I live, coming from another world—it seemed to me— so steady and easy, telling me that he loved us. Then in his quiet, detailed way, he told me what to do to get Bill going again. The practical, down-to-earth things. I never knew what a fine grown-up man I had married until that day. He made it seem not simpler but smaller—set against other people's trouble. It had happened; we could handle it. He had no doubt of Bill's strength, of mine, of his own; just love—and determination that nothing should keep Bill's life from being good and right for him.

"And all the time I was crying in the telephone, not saying a word."

For a moment she did not go on. Then:

"They kept him flying the Hump a long time in the last war. I was afraid he couldn't take it. But after he called me that day, I knew he could take anything. There is something in him that doesn't give an inch. It is as if he decided long ago what he values. I can't say it well—it is simply that he believes in life as people have to live it on this earth. He accepts it, not just the good part but death, trouble, pain, all of it. Not as evil which one must be resigned to but as experiences without which human growth would be inconceivable. When something happens, John doesn't waste a minute resenting it. He gets to work on it."

"And you?"

"Me. . . ." She sighed, and smiled quickly. "There are two: one does the wrong thing; the other runs fast to catch up and mend it. Always late. I've never been quite glued together. But you know that, don't you?

"Once," she said, "while things were hard, I thought of a talk we had, long ago, on the hill at camp. One Sunday morning. We were talking about our fears and dreads, learning to face up to a few of them. And someone asked you what you feared most—and before you could answer, they began to tell *you*."

One said, to have your face burned and left scarred. Another said, No; to be paralyzed would be worse; not to be able to dance. Another said it would be, for her, the forgetting of the past and her own identity. Another said she could take anything but the death of those she loved. One said she could not accept being poor—"losing our house and cars and my horse and all that; I'd rather be dead." And several agreed with her; they'd rather be dead, they said, than separated from their things. An older girl said, "It wouldn't be *things* for me. What would be hard for me would be to lose faith in the people I believe in. There are only a few," she said quietly, "but I need my belief in them."

Yes, I remembered that talk. And I had wondered, as we sat there together under the trees that Sunday morning, what life would ask these protected youngsters to take; where the breaks would come; out of what resources of intelligence and memory and belief and love, and hope, each would make her bridge. And Marty? Marty had said nothing. She was, as usual, playing with a beetle, or tickling the girl next her with a leaf.

"And all the time," she said now, "I was thinking of a woman who lived on the street back of us at home. She had lost her hand. It seemed to me the most dreadful thing: to lose part of your body. I remembered the old story about the woman with the golden arm—how she died and someone stole it from her grave and her ghost came back to earth searching for it. I suppose it means something different to each child who hears it. For me, it was a wind whistling around the darkest corners of my childhood. And as I sat there on the hill listening that day, it seemed too unbearable to speak aloud. And I thought, if anything like this ever happens to me, I'll die. It never occurred to me that—"

I thought she was going to refer to Bill's accident. But no. She said: "It never occurred to me that when something happens to you, *you* in turn happen to it. It is *you* who make the next move, *you* who decide what meaning the experience is going to have for you."

"You are wise if you have learned that."

"I haven't," she said with her quick candor, "not yet. I am still trying to learn."

She told me more of John's across-the-sea telephone calls to her, of his letters to Bill. Once, when things were rough for Bill, when he had gained enough of his strength to begin to look into a future he dared not see, she had written John of his discouragement and John called her from Tokyo and told her to tell Bill the story of Guillaumet.

"Guillaumet—I couldn't even remember who he was. And John said, 'Saint Ex's friend, darling!' As if they were his closest companions."

Antoine de Saint Exupéry. Of course. Though he knew him only through his writings, Saint Ex had been to John an intimate friend as he went on his lonely journeys through the sky. And Marty knew this. "But I could not remember about Guillaumet," she said, "I found the story in *Wind, Sand and Stars*, and that night I told Bill of Guillaumet's journey across the Andes, of his crash-landing in weather twenty degrees below zero, his walking his way out day after day, three days and nights, four—"

—Doing what no one thought he could do. He had come up from Patagonia, and with Exupéry and others in those early years of aviation he was opening up the first mail routes across the sky. They had been exploring the Andes, making their maps as they went across that vastness of snow and ice and silence. This day, he was alone. The sky did not look good; the winds were not friendly. But he had a job: to deliver the idea that in good weather or foul, mail could be brought across the Andes. And he went on, as those early pilots did, with few instruments to help him. It was not long before the way closed up behind him. Then it closed up in front of him. There was nothing to do but slog it out with the clouds, and he climbed as high as he could.

Then things began to happen: it was as if the winds had emptied the sky, leaving the plane in a vacuum; there was a moment when it seemed suspended between time and space then was caught and pulled like a slip of paper between the peaks and out again. He did not know how long the struggle had gone on when he felt the plane sucked down and rolled over and over like a hat in a road, he said afterward, from eighteen thousand feet to ten. Somehow he righted it and saw that he was trapped in a gorge flanked by sheer walls of ice and rock. At the bottom of it was a tiny glacial lake, beautiful and serene. He flew around it, again and again and again. There seemed nothing else to do. And he kept circling—until the petrol was exhausted and then he slid the plane down softly on the snow.

There was no way out except to walk and no path to follow and for two days the winds were too strong to walk against. So he sat in the shelter of his plane and waited. On the third day he began that incredible journey through snow, ice, along narrow ledges. He walked four days and nights. He had no food, the cold made him sleepy, the glare burned deep. It would be so easy to lie down.

Then the fight inside him began. All the forces gathered on one side or the other in battle for a man. His lungs wanted to stop breathing in the thin air, muscles stiffened, joints ached, hands grew numb, and he began to leave things: his knife, his glove, the equipment he needed to see him through. It was as if one part of him were ready to give up and die. But on the other side of the battle line, fighting back hard, were memories of his fellow-pilots, his wife; sudden scraps of talk, laughter; and belief that the sky belonged to men and men had to open it up, *he* had to open it up. If he failed now it would be harder for the others.

Another day passed. He was fighting his body's fatigue with two fixed ideas: his wife waiting . . . "she would expect me to come back"; his fellow-pilots waiting . . . "they would know I would keep on walking." So he kept on walking. But after a time he could not walk. He would lie down and sleep, he told himself, he had done all a man could do. It was at that moment that he remembered his insurance. His wife would not receive it for four years, according to French law, unless his body were found. She could not do without it four years. And he knew his body would not be found where he now stood, for when the snows melted in springtime it would be washed into a crevasse. Ahead of him, fifty yards ahead, was a large rock. If he could walk that far, his body would be found by shepherds when summer came. So he took a step, and another, and another.

When the peasants heard that his plane was down, they said it was impossible for him to come out of such ice and snow. "The Andes never give up a man in winter," they said. And Exupéry, who had flown to his assistance, believed it impossible, too, though he went up day after day to search for him. And other pilots searched. And somehow, though they knew it was impossible and said so, as they drank coffee together in the cafés of the Chilean towns, they expected Guillaumet to do it—as they would have expected themselves to do it, even though it could not be done.

"It became our bedtime story," Marty said. "Bill reserved a few lines for himself. *The Andes never give up a man in winter* —that was his to say." And always at the last—when Guillaumet was spotted near a remote village, having taken that one step and the next and the next, and Saint Exupéry had flown there and brought him back to the hospital in Mendoza and he lay half dead, starved and nearly blinded, with both hands frozen—it was Bill's turn to say those spine-tingling words when Guillaumet told Saint Ex, "I swear I have been through things no animal could come through!"

And each night after the story was done, Bill's mother said they would sit there without a word. Then Bill would say "Gee . . . and he walked out of something nobody could walk out of just because Saint Ex expected him to and those other pilots; he knew they did; and his wife expected him to—"

"—and he expected himself to."

And Bill would say softly, "Yep. That's it."

She told me of a letter John wrote on the eve of Bill's leaving the rehabilitation center. Bill had been there a long time, among people whose bodies had been stripped of strength or broken or altered by accidents or illness. He had grown used to that upswing of body and the soft down-thud of crutch on floor of a paralyzed girl walking down the corridor; to the people in wheel chairs working, playing, eating their meals; to the contour of men, women, boys, girls without limbs, to the metallic sounds of braces, locking, unlocking and the glint of prosthetic arms and legs; as used to all this as a medieval warrior was used to armor. But outside, he would be the only one on his street without arms; the only "cripple" in his schoolroom. He would be different. And that would be new; that would hurt.

So John wrote his son a letter. He told him, in words as simple and plain as those he used in making his reconnaissance reports, about a man's rights. He said he was fighting in Korea for those rights, for his own, for Bill's, for Marty's. "For everybody's rights, Son, no matter where they live. But sometimes a guy gets mixed up. You hear so much about rights these days you begin to think you have a right to everything. Even to a body with two legs and two arms and sight and hearing and so on. But you don't. No one has a right to that kind of body. It's a gift. God gives it to you or nature gives it, or you can call it the evolutionary process, or however you want to speak of it. In big words or little words, it is a gift. And not everybody is given it. For accidents happen before birth, as well as afterward. I know a great chap who was born without arms and legs. . . .

"And sometimes," he said in this letter, "even when we have a gift to begin with, it gets messed up. You know about that. And I know too, out here, because it has happened to some of the bravest men I've flown with. It's funny how a guy can get mixed up about things. He loses a leg, say; or his arms, or his sight; he begins to feel he hasn't had a fair deal; things are raw; he's been gypped; somebody's taken his right to a whole body away from him. He's all wet, Bill.

"But there is a right that you do have; everybody has; and that is the right to a whole life, whether you have legs and arms, or not; no matter how different you may be. And I mean by a whole life, a life full of fun and interesting experiences (along with the hard things), and people you love, and a girl some day, and a job you like to do, and sports, and making things better for others. We are going to do our best, Bill, to help you hold on to that right. To see that nobody takes it away from you. But you have to walk to it, boy, like Guillaumet. All your mother and I can do is stand by, and help when we can."

Bill read that letter to pieces. He did not comment on it. He handed it to his mother to read, then asked for it back and read it again and again. Marty could not be sure how he was taking it. Perhaps it is over his head, she thought. Maybe you can't understand about having no right to a whole body when you're just a kid. Then one day, Bill said to her, "I'd like to meet a man born without arms and legs. Gee . . . it must be wonderful to be born that way and yet learn to walk and do things."

"So we went on a little journey, too." Marty smiled. "We visited rehabilitation centers, talked to people who had 'done things no animal could do.' It was an amazing and humbling week for me—and thrilling to Bill. He was with friends. They spoke the same language, laughed at the same jokes. For weeks after we came home, he practiced them on Jenny."

One day, Bill said, "I guess I'll be an orthopedic surgeon. Don't reckon they'd let me fly a plane, do you?" he said, with careful casualness.

"They might," said Marty.

"Well, I may do both," said Bill. "Fly a plane and be a surgeon too. You see, if I was a surgeon, and somebody came in and had to have his arms off, he wouldn't get so scared if he saw that his surgeon didn't have arms either. I bet it'd help."

"I know it would," said Marty.

"Do you think I was wrong to say it?" she asked. "Maybe I have too much faith now, for anything seems possible to me, after this."

But there were nights when Guillaumet walking his way out of that twenty-below-zero trap in the Andes could not help; and John's letters could not help, and Bill's dreams of what he was going to be could not help. And Marty, in her room, across the hall, would hear the low sobbing begin. Sometimes she let him fight it out, knowing there is one kind of strength that can be found only within the lonely center of you. But at other times, she could not, herself, bear the loneliness and she would go in and sit by his bed and sing to him, binding him back to her, letting him be the little boy he had to be, now and then; and finally he would hush and she would hear him quietly breathing in sleep.

I looked at Marty as she sat there under the tree. No bigger than a young girl. Black hair shining in the light from the setting sun. Face, as elfin bright as when she raced over the hills at camp, but tired now, and with lines too deep—as if a make-up artist had prepared it for a role a little too heavy for her to play, a little too rigorous.

She stood up. "It has been a good afternoon. But we must go."

The sun was setting and she stood there a long time, looking toward that vagueness we call "Korea." "He is always so sleepy and grumpy in the mornings." Her voice was low. And then she ran quickly down the path toward the river.

The two were out on a rock in the shallows, close to a quiet pool. Bill had caught five fish, Jenny two. "It's Bill's hook,"

Jenny said. "It brings him luck. Look, he doesn't have to feel the worms. Ugh," she shuddered prettily.

"Silly!" Bill laughed and showed us how he managed the bait.

"There was a big guy at the center," he said suddenly, "eighteen years old. He was quarterback on his school team. He lost his hands above the wrist in a car wreck. They gave him a Krukenberg."

"What is a Krukenberg?" Jenny asked.

"It is what the surgeon does to give you something like fingers," Bill said.

"Fingers!" Jenny shrieked delightedly. "You mean the surgeon can make fingers?"

"You tell her," Bill turned to me. I felt an urgency in his voice. *He wanted Jenny to know.* So I told her the little I knew about this skilled and complicated operation, this plastic creation of "fingers" done by separating the two bones of the lower arm and rearranging muscles and tendons, flesh and skin, so that when it heals there are two long separate parts of the lower arm that have many of the functions of the human finger, especially that of feeling. "There are men who have lost their sight and their hands in accidents or in war and with their Krukenberg fingers are now reading Braille. It puts them back in touch with their world. They are able not only to read but to feel things once more: hard and soft things, and smooth and rough and warm—"

Bill was watching Jenny. The muscles of his face had tightened, giving him a quick and terrible maturity. And Marty's hands were locked together until the knuckles were white, and suddenly the victory, the peace which they had achieved seemed to slip away, and the raw struggle was laid bare—the never-ending pull of the human spirit against an irreversible fact.

"It's wonderful," Jenny said gravely, "to be able to feel things." And then she turned to Bill and said, "I wish you had a Krukenberg, Bill." But her face, as she said it, was full of pride and affection and I knew that her words were no more than if she had wished for him a million dollars.

"Oh well," said Bill quickly. "And what good would it do me at my shoulder, silly! Make me look like a drip, perched up there, wouldn't it?" He laughed and she laughed, and it grew funnier and they laughed more, and we laughed, too, with these crazy, wonderful kids whose nerves and minds and hearts jumped that chasm which had opened up suddenly in front of us and landed square on their feet.

After we came home, I sat in John's study reading Saint Exupéry's *Wind, Sand and Stars*. It had been a long time since I had read it. So long, that I had almost forgot the power of his masculine prose, the fine curve of an imagination that is as surrounding of thought as is a woman's. Like placenta, nourishing an idea a long time, until it is ready to be freed and comes forth sharply defined and alive.

Thinking, as I read, how impossible it is to read a book with one's own mind at the time of its popularity: one sees it, then, with its subtleties strained out; no nuances left in it. A million chewing readers too quickly make pabulum of it—and we remember, we actually taste on the page their reactions to it, rarely the words the author wrote.

The children were looking at television. Marty was preparing dinner. After a little, she called them to come help her finish things up. Bill set the table; Jenny beat a meringue—to such fine high peaks that she rushed in to show me. The Hump, she said, Bill's father used to fly over; it must be wonderful, she dreamed aloud, to fly over it at night and watch the sun rise— does it come up under you? like this? And then she tipped the Himalayas and they slid on to the rug and as we cleaned it up Bill came to the door to jeer at the mess and Jenny rubbed meringue in his face and Marty called them to go wash up, "If you're fighting her, Bill, watch out for your hooks."

It was impossible to believe that in this cheerful household there had ever been disaster, or could be.

## ❧ 13 ❧

A FEW weeks later, I picked up the morning paper and read of John's death. His plane had been shot down on a routine reconnaissance flight. A C-47 close by reported no parachute left the flames.

So a life ends. As if one had snapped a match in two. As if it were of no more consequence than a sliver of wood. This moment, when death seems to cheapen life by tearing out its bright purpose, is hard for the mind to endure. For Marty and Bill death was a hand against the throat—not an event to think about, write about. But I had never met John, and was detached, a little; and as I sat there reading the newspaper account again—as if it could give me the answer to the oldest question on earth!—my feeling was not one of sadness but of moral fatigue. Here was something that had seemed good to me; in this confused bitter world, here were three people who were creating together out of the chaos and pain of ordeal something that had goodness in it, and order, and peace. I felt that. And I had liked this family portrait which Marty's words and my memory of her summers in camp and a thousand memories of my own, maybe, were creating. And now it was as if a knife had slashed the canvas in two.

We had sat in his study that April evening. Jenny had gone home. Bill was asleep. Marty was smoking. I was reading and thinking about John as I read. It was natural for Marty to overesteem him—I had not forgot her passionate need of heroes when she was a little girl—yet I felt a large validity in what she had told me. I wanted to know about his childhood; how he felt about God: two questions that are rarely answered even when one can ask them. And yet, if one only knew the answers one would know a few of the experiences and beliefs at least, out of which come a man's strength and courage and tenderness.

The study was small—hardly more than a wedge cut out of the dining room. Its walls were lined with books. Poetry, philosophy, novels, science—books John had collected since he was a young boy. In a corner was a small varnished oak bookcase full of popular science books, and *Tom Sawyer, Treasure Island*—*his* kid books, not Bill's.

Near my chair was a shelf of technical journals and textbooks he had used at Yale and M.I.T. He was a civil engineer—his special interest was the designing and building of bridges. He had worked his way through college; in vacation as surveyor, as timekeeper, one summer as riveter on a bridge job. In between stints in the Air Force, he had helped as a young assistant to design a bridge which spans a finger of Chesapeake Bay. Now and then I drive over it on the coastal route from Georgia to New York: a fabulous swing it is when earth drops away and you see nothing but sky and steel, sometimes nothing but cloud, then water slides in front of you and you feel the ground come close and now it has turned into an ordinary bridge—if a bridge can be ordinary.

When he was on leave he had taken Bill to see it. He told him how the engineers studied terrain and winds and currents a long time before deciding to put it here. Once the spot was chosen, they went to work to learn how to build it. They knew how a thousand bridges had been built but they did not know how to build this one. "We had to learn everything we could about the laws of tension and stress or else winds and rocks and floods might outwit us."

"But if you knew how a thousand bridges were built," Bill had asked, "why did you have to study so hard?"

"Because each new thing you make is different," he told his son, "the curve is different; funny . . . how winds always blow across *your* bridge in a strange and different way. And materials are different. It is a different century, a different year."

"It is beautiful, like Bach," Marty had said.

"Did you mean to make it beautiful?" Bill asked.

And John, after a long time of looking at that great structure which seems to fly through space, said, "No. We wanted to build a bridge that people could cross—millions of them, in cars; there was space to span; dangers in the sea; materials had to be right, had to take a hard beating; we expected it to survive decades of use—we hoped, centuries. If it did, if it survived and served its purpose it would have beauty—its own kind, not something we added to it.

"That sounds good," he said after a moment, and looked at Marty and laughed, "but it isn't quite true. We might have designed it differently had animals or a creature from another planet been driving those cars."

"Gee, Daddy, spacemen?"

"But it was for earthmen," he told Bill, "with nerves and eyes

and brain and the memory of twentieth-century human beings"
—who drive cars, ride in planes not just to go places but for a
strange satisfaction you get when you leave something behind
that you've finished with (for a time, at least) and you feel
the earth dropping away . . . the sky coming close. . . . "No,
Bill, I am wrong. We did mean it. We hoped the folks who
drove over our bridge would feel what we felt when we
dreamed it up. We designed it that way. You see, we wanted
to take them further than just across the bay."

"That is the way John feels," Marty had said, "and the way
he talks to Bill."

I turned away from the shelf of technical books and searched
for Hart Crane's poems. The small book would be here, somewhere. Crane's *Bridge* did not take him even across the bay—
not quite; his dreams were too heavy for it and it failed to fuse
the poet and the person in him with life. The brilliant soaring
poem that never found its own deep meaning but trembled
suddenly and was shattered and lay on the "cruel bottom of the
sea."

I would have liked to talk with John. About bridges. About
this poem. About this symbol used by us in our dreams and our
books. Of all man's symbols (and how strange it is that he is
satisfied with so few) it ties us closest to death and life. A man
fails to find the capacity for love and the human being within
him begins to die; the bridge breaks. It has been said by so
many—by Kafka who wrote of nothing else for he could find
no bridge that could hold the weight of his life—said by Goethe,
by Lawrence, by Wilder, by so many others, again and again,
sometimes without the author realizing the meaning of what he
intuitively put down, so truly.

This kind of symbolic death, I understood; it seemed to make sense. ("Make sense": what feeble words for us to insist that the infinite universe conform to!) But the sudden death of people who *do* love, who *can* create what is good, who have bound themselves to life in ten thousand ways: when *their* bridge breaks—what meaning can we read into it?

Even on that quiet, peaceful evening, in John's study, that question lay ready to ask itself though I was thinking of life, not of death—of the bridge as symbol of ever changing life, of its binding power. For it is more than a symbol of infantile or incestuous love, of the wish to "return to the womb"; of death; more even than a symbol of mature love: It is the great metaphor of man's unceasing reach for the future, his never-ending mediation with the infinite. And I felt that John knew this in a way that I had not yet learned.

"John's feeling—his acceptance of life—where did he learn this?" I asked Marty.

She did not answer at once. "Not from—these," she said, looking at the book-lined walls of his study. "Not directly. What I have always felt in him is that he has no sense of alienation from his world. He is fused with it, with his family, his past, his future—but I said that, this afternoon."

"God?"

"He does not often talk about God. I think he has a profound feeling—something very humbling; but his mind is oriented by mathematics, mechanical engineering, aeronautics—he could no more talk the language of theology than he could use Chaucer's English. To me, he seems to belong to his universe. A grandiose way to say it, but he does. He doesn't fight it as if it were his mortal enemy. He accepts—not man's laws for he

knows how foolish they can be sometimes, but natural laws—
those science knows and does not yet know. He sees the human
being growing within this great framework of law, not beating
his brains out against it but using it to make life better for himself, maybe for everybody." She smiled quickly, "Of course I
am very much in love with John, and you should cut down to
size anything I say, but I think I am right: that to him science
is a great religious venture, not because science is to be worshiped or can take the place of God, but because he thinks
every new scientific discovery, every finding of old error, brings
men closer to the meaning of life. And if that happens, they are
closer to God. I think he has a very deep awe."

"Is awe enough?"

Marty did not answer for a long time. "I have spoken very
freely for him," she finally said. "More so than I have a right
to do.

"I think his sureness with life comes because he loves so
surely. But how does one learn to love like that? I almost hated
him, once, because of it."

And then she told me. It happened while John was at home:

She had wished for him every day. But when the news came
that he would have a four months' leave she began to dread it.
Things would be different. It was strange that Bill's losing his
arms could change her relationship with John and his with her
and theirs with Bill. But it had done so. This she suddenly knew.

The only part of this feeling that her mind could put into
words was her realization of the shock John would have when
he saw Bill. No matter how many facts he knew, his eyes had
not seen; a new image would take the place of the old; in one
instant would destroy it. To look on as this happened—

The night before his plane came in, she did not sleep much. Against a background of feelings impossible to fit to words flashed questions. Should she suggest to Bill that he wear his hands? Or let him do as he wished? He liked to wear his hooks, they were convenient but John was not used to—no, let him do as he wished. Should she have sent pictures? It would have been unfair. Maybe she should go alone to the airport, talk it over—but Bill wanted to see John too, it would not be right to leave him out of this important moment. But would John be able—

It kept on all night.

The next morning, early, she heard Bill up, walking around; now in the shower; now pulling out bureau drawers. He came into her room dressed to the hilt. Hair wet, slicked back with a high-smelling lotion on it. Neck scrubbed. One hand on; one hook. A big red handkerchief in his hip pocket. A purple tie. A yellow sweater. His school patrol badge.

"He was wonderful to look at," she said.

The morning was sunny and cold and fresh-blowing from the Sound as they drove to LaGuardia Airport. They had only a few minutes to wait. The plane was overhead; it taxied down the strip; passengers began to leave it. She was trembling all over. She would not look at Bill; it might be easier for him—for her—so she looked straight ahead. She saw John wave—and Bill was in front of her now waving back.

"Gee, Daddy's grown a lot," Bill shouted. And he did look taller than his six-feet-two as he stooped through the door of the plane and came down the runway. She laughed. And Bill laughed, realizing that he had said something funny and they were laughing when John came up to them. He took Bill by the shoulders, gave him a shake and kissed him, and said, "I got something for you." Then, "Gee, Bill, what you been doing to her! She looks wonderful." The things you'd expect a man to say. It was only when he took her in his arms that she knew he was trembling too. But it was all right. Everything was natural and right. "Why is it that we try so hard to hide our most decent feelings?"

They went to the car laughing and talking, now and then one of them wiped away tears. But no one minded. "We were just glad to be together." And they went home and had a big breakfast of waffles and ham and eggs, and Bill had a cup of coffee to celebrate.

For a few weeks they skidded along on sheer excitement. Then things happened. "One day I touched something very disagreeable in myself."

The feeling was quickly gone. John was in Bill's room at his worktable helping him. They were building shelves, planning to make a stool, many things. She thought *This is just what Bill has needed.* Then the feeling slid back over her. Across the whine of the electric saw, she could hear them talking. "Listen, Daddy," and Bill would talk talk to John. Talk, talk—as if he had been saving it up. *As if she could not understand,* she whispered the words to herself. "Had I screamed them I could not have been more shocked."

The next day she was cleaning John's study, running the vacuum over his shelves. Their voices kept coming through. *Listen Daddy.... Boy, you're somep'n ...* thin voice, deep voice. *But Dad, you see....* She could not hear all the words but she tried to. "I cleaned those books a hundred times as I stood there, snooping on my two."

She had had Bill to herself so long. All the pain and responsibility—and satisfaction had been hers. It had not been easy, she had made plenty of mistakes, she knew. But she had brought him through; he was doing all right. Now she felt as if her job had been taken over by a superior officer.

"The point was, I knew John would do a better job than I had. And it burned me up." She had never been jealous before —of anyone as far as she could remember. But it seemed so easy for him—coming home—seeing Bill—she felt she had worried unnecessarily about, well, everything. And now Bill had turned to him. She wasn't in the picture—

It seemed impossible to accept this new look at herself. Bill needed John's humor and ease and masculine know-how. Without it, he would not learn what a man can be. A boy must have this image. This was clear to her. Her brain had not shrunk. "It was my heart," she said, "I had not known I could be so small."

She put away the vacuum, left a note, took the car and went out to the river where we had been on this day. Where John and she had gone many times; where they used to camp in the summers; long ago he had told her here, as they cooked over a campfire, of his dreams to go to M.I.T.; and she had told him one cold windy day as they walked along the river's edge that she was pregnant; and when his mother died they had talked about his childhood under the same old trees. All the little things not thought of for years had tumbled out that day, his memories, hers. Everything, almost, in their life together had been talked over, out here. "I guess I thought it would come back; if I could see the trees, the old rock, I'd see the whole design, maybe, and fit this piece in with the rest. Maybe it would not seem so evil to me. But I could not think it through. All I could hold to was the knowing that if I began now to compete with John for Bill's love and esteem, it would tear our lives up. Bill would lose something far more important to him than his arms."

"You knew that?"

"Yes—but I was resentful. I was more resentful for now I was fighting myself *and* John."

After hours of sitting there on that cold day—"I remember the sun had gone down"—she found herself trying to pray. Desperately. Foxhole praying. "But I wasn't in a foxhole. I was surrounded by people who could help me. It was a long time, though, before I realized that.

"I suppose I wanted something magic to happen. At once. And it didn't."

She had not prayed since she was a child. Not even when Bill was hurt. "I knew nothing of prayer. Mother and Dad go to church; they think nice people do. But what religion or prayer means to them, I have no idea."

"You see, God meant nothing to me." When she was a little thing, the word was shadowy and floaty. "Magic, sort of," she smiled, "like mushrooms popping up in the night, and double rainbows, and icicles on a cold still moonlit roof. Wonderful and dreamlike." As she grew up, God turned into a hard abstraction. Something you don't feel but you talk about. "After the war, my little crowd talked a great deal about God—I am afraid, because it was the thing to do." As they discussed Russia and Marx, and the Chiangs, or Freud, or Jung or Einstein, American demagogues, England's socialism, or Gandhi, or Menotti's operas. "We read Existentialism—Sartre, the others; I even plowed through Kierkegaard, and Karl Barth. John

kidded me; but I did. And a friend of mine went in for Yoga."
Talking about God . . . trying on his various wondrous gar-
ments as if it were a fashion show, to see which one became
them most. War-hurt and conditioned by science; talking talking but afraid to feel; not relating themselves to Him.

"I had never experienced God," she said very simply. "I don't
think you do until you feel you must see a few inches around
the curve—

"But that day, at the river, I wasn't thinking about God. I was
shocked and scared. I wanted something but I didn't know
what."

"Has prayer helped you find it?"

She was sitting on a stool near the bookshelves. She picked
up one of Albert Schweitzer's books, turned the pages as if she
were going to read something to me, laid it down. "Not that
day. Now it means to me—stillness. A stopping of the noises
inside—the awful pull of my feelings and mind in different directions. If I can only grow quiet—then I feel that maybe I
have prayed, a little. I'm learning not to ask favors. I cannot
believe a relationship with God is a dole system. It doesn't sound
very holy, but prayer, to me, is a kind of cleaning out of my
bureau drawers, throwing away what I no longer value, holding on to what is important to me, and to Bill and John—and
maybe a lot of others whose names I do not know.

"I've discovered that only a few things really matter. Just a
few."

"Isn't it strange," she said after a time when neither of us
wanted to say more, "that I could have envied John the very
qualities I love in him and depend on?

"Envy is hardly the word—I hated him that day. It seemed

to me he had done everything right from the beginning of our trouble. He had made no mistakes. And I had made so many! I knew I would make more—and some of them would be hard for Bill to forgive and for me to forgive. I hated John because of his success. I knew it came because of his capacity for tenderness and concern, and I hated him for that, too. I ached that day with the unfairness of it!

"Bill isn't the only cripple in our family. I've learned that."

"All of us are crippled," I reminded her. "John is. Everybody. We cannot forget that."

"Oh I know, I know," she said quickly, "but don't tell me it evens up."

She knew I did not think it "evened up." How could it! We are not sums of arithmetic but people, different in psychic resources, in health, in ten thousand fascinating ways. And not one of us is without blindness and deafness, and moral paraplegia, and broken relationships, and retarded imagination— If we could only accept our differences! Whether of body or mind or emotions or beliefs—

"But maybe it wasn't all jealousy. I saw something, that day, I had never been willing to look at before. Ever since I was a kid, I have used insight as my defense; it seemed to me it could help me through anything. If I could only understand . . . could see into the trouble, could get the facts. . . . But I realized, that day, that insight is to love what cineplastic arms are to real ones. A makeshift; a pitiful makeshift; wonderful, yes—until you remember living arms."

"I've known you a long time. Your image of yourself is not the one I have of you."

I can still see her, that little black-headed girl in green shorts, racing down the rock steps, to the swimming pool, the stables, the tennis court, into the clay room, lying on the hill in the twilight listening to music, or climbing peaks with the big girls, dreading the cliffs, the snakes, but wanting to go; eager for life and so terribly afraid of it. It was not one fear or two or three, though it would begin that way: She would be afraid to swim at the deep end of the pool, maybe—then what would happen? That fear would draw another fear out of her, less specific, more shapeless, and another, and another. . . . It was like reading a biography backward to watch her fears creep out until even her baby fears were there too, and they were the giant ones, of course, and suddenly it was not a pool in a girl's camp with lifeguards every forty feet around it—it was a great uncharted sea full of terrors—and yet even then she wanted to swim it. How often I had seen the little fears gather and mass into a formless anxiety which no nine-year-old child could deal with. And when it happened, she would be blocked off from her courage, love, enthusiasm, her sense of humor, her irrepressible desire to experience. But not for long. Something in her would get to work on that great boulder blocking her way. I have watched her so many times. She did have insight, even as a small child, a very special talent for it; and, mixed with her refusal to fail, it ate that boulder away like an acid, until she could get around it, and in contact again with her love, her genuine feeling for people and life.

"I cannot see it as lack of love," I said. "Isn't it fear? All your life, your insight has helped you tolerate anxiety. I'd call it a fine prosthetic aid. And everybody has to have a few, remember."

"But that day my foundations were rocking."

"What did you do?"

She laughed. "I went back to my new enemy, John, for help. It is ridiculous but it is what I did."

They were waiting for her when she came in, that evening. They had cooked dinner and set the table and were in the kitchen trying to figure out a way to keep the food warm. The kettle was boiling and John was saying, "Now what do you think of trying a little hot water under the shrimp, Sergeant?" She stood at the door a moment, looking at them. Each had on one of her aprons, faces were flushed, they looked as if they had had quite a workout—

"But we don't have to warm it up," yelled Bill, "she's here."

"Hi," said John, as if she had just stepped around the corner to the store. And Bill, taking his cue, said, "Hi."

And then she helped them take up dinner. When they went into the dining room she saw that they had put a few red roses in her little white bowl—the one she kept in her bedroom because she loved to look at it. And she felt warmed by this wordless effort they were making and close to tears for a moment. But John kept it easy and gay and casual by telling her the small absurd events of the day. And as they sat there, eating the shrimp stew he had made, she realized how thin he had grown since his return and how tired, really tired, Bill looked —worn-out from trying to stretch up as tall as his father. And she knew suddenly that they had found it as hard as she: each had been hurt by a different thing, maybe, had suffered in a different way, but battle fatigue was on all their faces.

After supper, they played Canasta. When it came time for Bill to go to bed, he told them good night and went to his room.

And she and John sat there, smoking, not talking, now and then smiling at each other, questions in John's eyes—she did not know what was in hers.

And then Bill called her. He was standing in the middle of his room. He had taken off his arms though he still had on most of his clothes. As she walked in, he sort of grinned and waited a moment, then said very low, "Mommy, will you help me to bed?" And she knew as if he had written her a long letter how he felt about her, and about John. She winked at him and said, "Sure," and then he ran to her and began to cry hard trying to smother the sobs against her shoulder, so his father would not hear. After he was in bed, she sat by him, stroking his hair now and then, and he stared out the window and did not say a word.

When she went back to John he was in the study smoking his pipe, and reading.

She wanted to tell him at once all that had troubled her. But he began to tell her what had troubled him:

It was not so hard in Korea, he told her, to take it. About Bill. He could see it, out there, set against the suffering of the whole world. It was his boy, yes; and he hurt for him; and for her; but there was distance—the distance that comes not as much from geography as from a totally different setup where the size of personal disaster changes, somehow. He could be philosophic about it out there—enough to keep his bearings, keep his mind clear. But when he came home, and saw, actually saw Bill—"I became a little boy, too, I reckon." He had to fight harder than he had ever fought against storm or mountain or the enemy—and there she was, he said, going about things easily, calmly as if nothing had happened. He'd watch Bill put on his arms—his daily routine—"and the sweat would pour out of me and she would be telling Bill to hurry, the others were waiting, voice casual, easy," he wrote a friend in Korea, who sent her the letter after John's death. "I was a raw recruit and she the veteran, taking it, determined to treat him like a boy, not like a cripple—and not like a hero either. And as I watched her I was humbled by this courage of women—only the word is not courage, precisely, nor is it creativity; our language has no word for it because, perhaps, we do not yet know it for what it is: they go about so quietly cutting tragedy down to a size that they can fit into a home. And we? we males set it on a stage, turn all the lights on and strut our little piece—or else we wholly deny it. And sometimes we make great poetry of course, but they make life. And what is better than life, Bob?"

"I am not in the least like that," Marty wrote me, "and most women aren't. Though his mother was, a little. But I like to believe John thought so."

He said that night only enough for her to understand how he felt about her and Bill. But she knew he had guessed her trouble so truly that there was little more for her to say.

"It was then that we began to feel it, think it together"—to see how one's problems change as one's framework changes. John's problem changed when he came close to it. Then it was that it slipped from his mind where he could handle it objectively, into his heart and blood stream and nerve endings, and he suffered as if the accident had happened that day. And she had acquired her problem by maturing a little: along with this new independence, came a new pride. She had invested heavily of herself in their ordeal—it was natural for her to want to clip the coupons. "But neither of us could clip them, rightfully; only

Bill," she said. "And not even Bill." That night they began to see this: to see that somehow theirs and Bill's trouble must be shared with the world, just as one shares one's good fortune: They had to identify with all children who had lost their arms; had to give of their hurt and experience to help these others; had to do something to make it more difficult for accidents to happen; had to fuse their unique ordeal with every man's ordeal. Only by doing so, only by assuming the heavier burdens of mankind could they bear the light weight of their own.

"Things have leveled off now," she said. "When John comes home, we are going to do something—I don't quite know what—but something to help all children. We want to, we feel we must.

"But you will think me unteachable," she smiled, "when I tell you I still wish there could be a happy ending, though I know there can't be."

"But something—more real?"

"Yes," she sighed. "Maybe. Understanding . . . sympathy . . . (the words came slowly as if heavy with nights of thinking) acceptance . . . knowledge . . . forgiveness—all the learning that gives men their flavor and strength—you don't know how often I say the words to myself, trying to believe them."

We did not talk more. She said good night and went to her room. And I stayed in the little study thinking about her, and looking at John's books.

This I remembered as I read the newspaper that morning which told of John's death. It came back to me, in bits, in fragments that made no pattern, no wholeness. For it seemed

to me, then, that John's death had not only torn the purpose
out of his and Marty's lives but that it made all life weaker than
death—that it placed every man's dreams and hopes and plans
at the mercy of death. And I could not, for a long time, see beyond that. And because I could not, I found no way of com-
posing these fragments.

But I know now. Death can kill a man; that is all it can do
to him; it cannot end his life. No.

Because of human memory. Because of words. Because of
symbols. Because he uses his hands and brain not only to fight
the enemy but to make things; to create, to discover new
knowledge. Because his dream does not die with him, nor
his relationships, nor his knowledge, but is left in that great
reservoir which Timothy loved to talk about, of human experience on which we draw—all of us—every day of our lives, and
on which our children will draw, and their children. We have
been dipping into it, into this great sea around us, this limitless
sea of experience for a quarter of a million years. We take from
it what we need, metamorphosing it into something new and
different by our relationship with it, we use it and then we die
. . . and our lives and dreams and hopes and words go back in
it, deepening it, enlarging it. Our triumphs and our failures
go in it—and the human beings who live after us are nourished
on both; sometimes, perhaps, growing more from our failure
than from our success. Sometimes this is so and it eases the heart
to remember it.

Immortality? I do not know how to talk about it save in
words that have come from our earthly experience. For we have
words only for what we have experienced either in dream or

actuality between birth and death or what another human being has experienced, or ten billion have experienced. Mathematical, theological, scientific formulae do not help me here.

But I take comfort in the immortality of the human memory —in its power to conserve all that has happened to us, and our power to record, to use, to create out of it something utterly new by discovering new meanings in old wisdom and in old hurts and old beauty. And because human beings have this miraculous power, I believe there is laid upon them a responsibility to make use of it by extending their personal memory into their past lives as far as they can go and by reaching back into the history of the human race to find what is there, gathering it up, all of it they can, to be used by others in the making of man's future.

And because of this great and wonderful gift of memory, we can hold on to a relationship after the person with whom it was formed is dead. And sometimes, for the first time, we then understand its meaning. For death releases it from the bondage of time. It is freed, it becomes four-dimensional, irrelevances are sloughed off, it begins to come clear, and we can see it whole. The wonder of it is that it continues to grow as long as we grow.

And that is what, I think, will happen to Marty and Bill.

They will not forget John: they still have that relationship, they still have their knowledge of him, and the experiences they shared with him they will still remember; and it will go on and on in their lives and what they do and think and feel will always have something of John in it.

In this sense, there is always a resurrection. . . . A man dies: on the third day, after the mourning is over, he is resurrected in the minds, in the memories and hearts of the people who love him, who experienced him, and he will always stay there, and become part of them. And if he is the kind of man John was—because John did raise the level of human experience, did lift it a few inches—they will try to keep the level there. They will be proud that there are human beings, a few like John, who can accept life so completely, can love so without conflict as John was able to do, and take great risks for what they believe in, as John did.

Bill will not forget this. Nor Marty. And they will be able to go on with their lives, perhaps live them with more strength than they would have done had not John died, for they might have depended on him, too much.

It is the old story: the story of death and resurrection. Out of which grew the Christian ritual of the Lord's Supper. Very primitive and very old—and very true. True of every relationship: that what is real in it gets finally into us, into our minds and lives, almost as if we had—eaten it.

It does not give life a "happy ending" to believe this; but it gives it significance. And it gives meaning to death, for we begin to understand the creative role it plays in life, in our life, in all human experience. It is a curious thing: we can think of death without life but we cannot think of life without death; the ten thousand little deaths are always there and it is out of them that more life comes. The old sloughs off; the new shoot grows. We see it clearly not in one life or one generation but in two, three, in ten. As the lengthening curve of time is revealed by personal memory, by history, we see it more and more clearly.

I do not think life and death are giants struggling for supremacy over the human being and that, finally, death always wins. No. This concept makes good theater; it made Greek tragedy; it made vivid, even hypnotic, the writings of the German philosophers; it made the Faustian bargain; it has fathered terrible and beautiful poetry. But if you remember time, if you think beyond the space of one man's years, you know it is not true. Life always wins; always goes on. There is an old Negro song: *Death is a little man—* And that is right. The African slaves knew more about the curve of time than did the Greek poets: the "little man" can never end a human life; he is not big enough.

But there is a way in which Marty and Bill can destroy their relationship with John: if they turn their memory of him into an image and bow down to it.

We mortals can effect an annihilation which death is not capable of. And how often we do it—to our gods, to our past, our parents, to great art and literature and great events and to our most precious beliefs: killing what we cherish by turning it into the Absolute and worshiping it; cutting off forever the possibility of its entering us and through our lives growing and changing and becoming a part of the future of men.

*Make no graven images.* Never has a wiser admonition been given men. The trouble is that in our perverse way we have often chosen to misinterpret it. And feeling a falseness in this misinterpretation—for we know that sculptured images both of symbolic and natural subjects have given an incalculable enrichment to our world and only the ignorant think otherwise—we have discarded the deep meaning of this warning. For it is so true that a graven image set up within ourselves and worshiped becomes a shrine to our own death.

## ~ 14 ~

WHAT A generation does with its past is surely the most crucial decision it makes, for on that choice depends the shape of its future.

And what one does with one's personal past is as decisive in a life. Worship it, hoard it, cling to it by forgetting as a child holds its doll in sleep, cling by hiding with it in bitterness and shame, cling by pinning it on like a medal: and one is as cut off from the future as was Lot's wife. Then death wins. Little man that he is, we are even smaller having had no real life of our own. But when the past becomes for us the living word, when we use it as the limitless resource it is—evaluating, selecting, transforming it until it becomes fluid enough to get into mind and imagination and blood stream—then it nourishes a new life within us that links on to the future and cannot be destroyed when we die.

And it is a hundred times a day in small and silent ways that we decide how we shall live with our past, not in one final illuminated decision with the trumpets and bass viols blasting away.

Ordeal . . . change . . . death . . . the end. How easily our feelings tie them together in a sequence that spells only disaster. We know that out of ordeal comes the new growth, out of change comes the new way, we know life would stop without the ordeal that brings the change, we know death does not end a man's life—our intelligence has no doubt about it—and yet, most of us wish we could escape the experiences these words hold. The rest of mankind cannot. Of course. But in a secret corner of us we keep hoping that maybe we can.

Perhaps it is the word *inescapable* that breeds our fear. For it builds up a picture of a rendezvous which in a fatal and dread way we are compelled to meet. The old legend of the "appointment in Samarra" still haunts our minds with its half-truth, and drains the strength from us.

If we could only see these archetypal events not as disasters over which we have no control but as creative processes in which we make choices and decisions, if we could accept them as valid relationships whose quality we determine even though we cannot bargain away the pain—then we might find more easily their meaning for us and those who live after us. There *is* an end in death and ordeal; there is an end in change; there is an end even in birth—a very painful one; but there is also a beginning. And it has been by remembering this beginning that man has pulled himself into his unique place in the universe.

I believe every good life has a good relationship with death. Just as it has a good relationship with birth. There is a connection here. If we accept the profound significance of human birth, if we can think steadily and long on its meaning, if we can in our imagination go back to that primal moment and look with wisdom and tenderness at the joy and satisfaction and pain and travail of the separation which takes place between mother and child; if we can see how the life-pattern grows as each, cut loose from the other, begins to form new and different relationships with the self and the world and the people in it; how each turns to new ways of meeting its needs and yet still longs for the old way, a little: if we can accept the triumph and the agony, the anxiety and the tenderness and the wonder of this profound experience which holds within it both a tie and a separation, a life and a death and a new life, we can accept and understand it as the prototype of all human ordeal.

There is something canny in us which makes us know that those of us who fear death most are those who have feared life most. If anxiety has cut one off—not only from the satisfactions which come from successfully meeting one's hard moments but from the even more profound satisfactions of continuous growth, of moving steadily from one peak of human development to the next until we have come through the "eight stages," as Erik Erikson calls them, during which we meet our greatest difficulties and find our greatest opportunities—if fear has blocked our way, we feel that we have not, quite yet, begun to live. We keep hoping we shall begin—and now death is close, perhaps, and so little time is left. The second and the third and the fourth chance that fear withheld from us we now beg death for.

How often have we seen a homesick child act out this old drama. A seriously homesick child at camp or school, as most of us know, is the child who brought her "sickness" from home along with her tennis racquet and duffel bag and trunk. And it falls upon her with a new sharpness in new surroundings. She feels that if she could only get home, back to the past, everything would be fine: she would somehow, in a beautiful fairy-tale way, receive the acceptance and tenderness she feels she has not had; somehow the dilemmas which have not been solved and are keeping her from finding her identity would fade away; her second chance would be there waiting for her (and for her family)—if only she could get back. Having failed in many of her home experiences, she feels that she will surely fail again in this strange place! And some of us know that we look at every change in our life, even the Big Change, much as this child lost within herself does.

But there are people, enough of them to keep the old world a going concern, who have lived so deeply and with such rich satisfactions that death is only the rounding out of their life. Many of these have found a trusting relationship with their own mortality through their relationship with God. Others, who use a different language and think in a different mode, have found the same trusting relationship. They do not fear death. They do not fear because they do not feel that when they die they will be severed from the future. Each, with a different picture gallery in his imagination, using different words to say it in, speaks his faith that he will still be bound to the destiny of men and will still be a part of this wondrous thing we call human experience. It is a lovely thing to see: the person who accepts death with dignity just as he accepted life and its changes out of which he was wise enough to know had come his significant experiences.

There are two kinds of ordeals, of course: those we choose and those that seem to choose us. And some of these, like flood and hurricane and war, are so impersonal and large and awful that we feel we are only a piece of printed paper caught up in the hollow of its energy. And yet, even then, there are some who turn the print on their bits of paper into immortal words by their acts of courage and selflessness.

The ordeals we choose (and I refer now not to those we label "accident-proneness" or to the other varieties of self-punishment or self-reward) are those we accept because we know they are a necessary part of the journey to a place we want to go. One chooses to write a book and accepts with that choice the labor and uncertainty and self-searching and mind-ache which are necessary to carry it through to the end. An artist knows the ordeal of bringing from within him the formless dream, giving it shape and texture and color, turning a thousand amorphous bits of experience into an organic meaningful whole that can speak in dialogue with his world. Every mother knows. Every scientist and engineer. Athlete and dancer understand why rigorous discipline is necessary. A businessman who has dreamed and created a great industry knows the inevitable grind. All who live purposefully accept ordeal—the pain and the risk of it—as an integral part of the experience. This we take for granted unless we are sick or profoundly confused. We know it as the germinal event it is.

But the ordeal forced upon us carries with it a sense of violence and rape. We feel it not as an impregnating experience but as one in which something precious and inviolate has been torn from us. And we are filled with anger and resentment and shame, or worse, a terror that can teach us nothing—

Until we remember: that even though the mother may choose to bear her child, the child has not asked to be born. Both kinds of ordeal are locked together in human birth and both are locked together in life. And the quality of both is determined not only by the one experiencing them but by the people close to that one.

For we are never alone in ordeal. Although loneliness is

always with us and a hard thing to bear, even so, we are not alone. The airman forced down in the desert or in the wasteland of high mountains is not alone. He has a lifetime of memories and beliefs as his companions; a lifetime of resources within himself to draw upon, and the knowledge, like a flare in the dark, that there are people who care. And he knows that how he meets his ordeal is important even though no one is there to see and even though he may not survive it: for the seed of honor lies at the center of it and he cannot let it die, because of them. Because of the rest of mankind. Because of a future that has not yet been born.

This is true, even of the loneliest of ordeals: that which one suffers when holding to a belief which no one else seems to share—a belief which in folk speech is "ahead of its time." Even then, one is not alone: for never has a man held an ideal that was "ahead of its time." Always it is shared, silently, by innumerable others, in distant times and faraway places, or by the man next door. Somewhere in minds and hearts it is there: it may be a dry seed that has not begun to germinate but it is there; it may be sprouting greenly but not yet ready to be brought forth in word and act, but it is there. And these people care. And there will come a time when all men will care.

"What is there in a man that makes him know there is something bigger than he is?" he asked. "I wish I knew. Because I have seen it working. One man has it. Ten men don't. Yet sometimes in a split second that one man can give it to the ten. What is it? It would be easy to wrap it up in the word *religion* but a lot of things have been wrapped up in that word which I don't like."

We were sitting in a café in the Fifties, just off Madison Avenue. We had met at a CBS radio program on which we had appeared. It was the early spring of 1946. He had been a prisoner of war in Germany. Had been home only a brief time. I had a play on Broadway. I told, on that program, stories of the children in our play who ran into a few jagged facts of life while on the road tour of the show and what they did about it. He was a paratrooper. He had a mission to perform, left the plane over Germany. It was of what he thought on that slow journey down to earth when his parachute failed to open that he talked: of his old grandmother and her farmhouse; of the cow munching, switching her tail, looking back now and then as he stood there listening to the milk streaming into the pail; smells of the old barn; wisps of hay on Grandma's skirt. All this he remembered as he fell. "How slow you fall," he said. "It seemed quite a long journey, somehow." The steady plodding walk of Grandma back to the farmhouse, past the chicken house, its smells; past the woodpile, its smells. Grandma's deep easy voice as she asked him to carry in a load of wood. Twilight. Smoke coming out of the chimney. The kitchen stove, hot. Something good sizzling in frying pan. "Grandma had just begun to take up supper when my chute opened and I saw the ground rising up to meet me." When he woke up he was in a barn. A cow was munching. And all the right smells and sounds were there. But not Grandma. A pretty German girl was rousing him. He had fallen in a near-by field. She found him, got him with the help of someone (she would not tell him who helped) into the barn; and cared for his broken leg and fed him until he was discovered. The rest of the war he spent in a prison camp. The rest of his brief story was about his experiences there. He had made it a light and funny story, even as one felt the gravity beneath.

But now he was deeply serious as he asked that question. "The obscenities, the experiences so inhuman you can't find a word for them—things all of us in prison camps knew—don't nag me much. What keeps dragging at me is this: there are men in a tight spot who do the decent thing, there are others who don't. Can't. And this interests me. I'd like to know why.

"There we were," he said, "dumped together. Wired in. Each with a past no one knew but himself, and Lord, a lot of them didn't even know their past, maybe. Facing each other. Cut off from the whole universe. The future was a word you'd almost choke a man for saying out loud."

Stripped clean. "Well, maybe not quite." They had their memories. And some had a thousand times as many as others seemed to. And skills. And bits of beliefs. A little knowledge. And that quality we call character. And with what was left them they began to build a new world behind those walls. "Had to, or die. You just had to." But now and then a man didn't have to and stopped trying, and died—taking any means to die that he could lay his hands on.

But most chose to live. "Because there were a few men in there who kept us wanting to live." So they got busy. Tin cans, bits of string and paper, mud, and memories, "that's what we used to make things with. We just had to have something to look at. One guy made mobiles out of strings and bits of tin cans. Pretty good, too. And the rest of us would stare at them by the hour." They made rules and customs for themselves. "Had to. We needed them as much as things." And after a while there was a little something piling up in the emptiness.

"Nothing much happened—how could it! But we'd take what did and build it into headlines."

There were the rattraps. The men made them out of tin cans and laid bits of food in them. They had a system. It worked like this: If a rat was not too greedy he could nibble at the edge of the food without putting his body inside the half-cut lid and could escape being trapped. But a greedy rat would lunge in for all of it and wham—the lid had him. The men felt a profound justice in this. "We developed a sort of rat ideology. A greedy rat caught by the lid—too bad, but he got what was coming to him. A good guy who was not greedy—it was fine to watch him escape." The traps became an infallible test of the moral quality of rats. All the rats in the world they divided into rats who are greedy and rats who are not. The good rats they made pets of, tried not to mind when they nibbled clothes and ate the rations outside the traps.

Except Hector. Hector took up for the greedy rats. One night he made a speech in their defense. "He converted a half-dozen of the men to his side, too."

"A rat's got to be a realist," said Hector. "Look after himself. Who else going to look after him? Survival of the toughest, see? All this talk of the other fellow. Christ—you'd better take it while you can get it. When I get home, you watch me, I'm gonna get rich in two years. Velvet lined."

"Yeah but they don't survive—can't you see the dead rats every morning?"

"One did," said Hector.

"But look, Hector," said Jim who before the war was a professor of history at Dartmouth, "all history proves—"

"Aw jeez, rats aint in history. Where you go to school?"

"P. S. 116," said Jim.

"That explains it," said Hector.

"It was inside just as it is outside," said the young paratrooper, grinning. He ordered a drink.

Of small significant things like rattraps and big insignificant things like death was woven the fabric of their days. He told of a Russian Jew who was sent in to their camp with a work squad of Russians to do a special job. This Jew begged to stay. Russian Jews, he said, were treated worse than American Jews. He told them a lot. And the Americans let him stay and hid him by digging a hole under one of the cots where he crouched when the guards were around and slept at night there by sitting in an upright position in the hole. For two weeks it worked nicely. Then one day the prisoners were mustered out. The dogs sent in. They found the Russian as he huddled in his hole and tore him to pieces scattering bones and flesh over the floor while the Americans listened outside. "We never knew who told. But Hector had two packages of cigarettes, next day."

As he talked a waiter brought food to the table next to us. "That is more food than I saw in two months over there," the paratrooper said quietly. "And people are still hungry. But I guess you have to starve to know what starving is."

"The dogs ... you tell that story to me and I shut it off quick to keep from feeling too much. But when you were right there?"

"We turned our backs, too. Had to. No one ever mentioned it. Life was, well—there just wasn't much of it around. We knew it was a good idea to keep it in sight, if we could. Sometimes, if you thought too much about the way a man died it made it easy to let go—and die too."

He told me of the rules they made. There was the strict rule that you could tell your troubles only once. One time, each man could tell how his plane crashed, or his chute opened too slow, how he got caught, how he was hurt. After that, if he told it, he had to give a cigarette to each listener. Only a non-smoker usually felt it worthwhile to repeat the journey into misery at such an inflated price. But if the tale had to be told, then a man told it, and gravely passed a cigarette to each listener who gravely smoked his reward for having participated in the therapy.

There was the rule, too, about escapes. If a prisoner wanted to escape he presented his plan. If the men decided it was good, they agreed that he could make his try. They'd wish him luck, watch him slip away, knowing that each of them would pay for it by confinement, by being deprived of food; and things worse. A month of punishment might be the price extorted for one man's freedom. And no one minded as long as there was fair chance to escape. "But we were tough with those dreams," he said.

And then he asked it again. "What is it? What gives a man the strength to do it? To keep believing in life when death is all around? To act as if there is something important and you can't forget it even though you know you can't get out of the trap? It's a curious thing," he said, "to watch men caught in the same spot either not move at all or move out of it in such different directions. One toward hell-raising. One seems to get an understanding he'd never had before. One hates—just hates—all day long. One wants to come back home and make life easier for other people and dreams about doing it. In my camp there was one like that—I had the feeling that maybe he didn't suffer even hunger. He was way off, somewhere. Another wants to make life easy for himself. One talks about helping German kids escape the life their parents lived; another wants every German kid to pay twice over for his parents' sins. The vengeful ones sometimes have the most education."

We did not look for answers that night and did not find them.

But we talked a long time about the meaning men give to their experiences. That is something no animal can do. It may be trapped and wounded; and it will inevitably die. But it is not aware of the meaning of being trapped nor of the meaning of a wound, nor aware of its approaching death. And because it is not aware of these experiences it is not aware of life, either. It cannot savor it, however grimly it may hold on to it.

"That was Hector," the young paratrooper laughed. "Hector held on like a brute."

We talked of frustration. We agreed that frustration without meaning will kill a man, or drive him mad, or make a criminal of him. But if he can give meaning to the frustrating experience, it will nourish him and he will actually grow on it. But *he* has to give it its meaning.

"Like Steve," he said. "Steve found meaning in everything that happened. A cockeyed sort of fun, sometimes; Steve was like that. But somehow, he always got on top of it and made it do something for us. And because he did, it did even more for him. At least, it seems so now, as I think about it. Had a nerve like—well, you want to use words like steel, iron, but you're all wrong when you do. There was nothing in Steve like a machine. It was amazing how he could sense a man's mood and get in step with it. He kept us going. Now why? What was it?

"Anyway, it was something in Steve that—well, for instance

the day the dogs were sent in. There we were, outside. And
Steve's face was steady—sure—human—decent—and above it,
somehow. As if he had it all cupped together in his mind:
Nazis and Russians, war and dogs and man's cruelty and fear—
and a future when all this would be in the past. He had it and
he was on top of it. I reckon he hypnotized a lot of us for we
didn't take our eyes off him. He gave his last five cigarettes
away. I'm telling you, any man who can do that—"

We laughed and relaxed, a little. And ordered something to
eat.

"And there was Preacher. Preacher was the chaplain. He's got
a church now out in a little town in Iowa. Preacher and Steve
were quite an outfit.

"It's not so easy as the word 'maturity'—people seem to be
using it nowadays—might lead you to think," he said soberly.
"What they did. Something made them feel responsible for
keeping alive the best that men have learned about how to come
through a tough spot.

"And Jim. Professor, we called him." He laughed. "Craziest
fool alive. He lost his leg—cut half off by his plane's propeller,
he thinks—he jumped—it was night and he was over the Medi-
terranean—chute wouldn't open—he and the plane got too close
together for a second—then he fell like a piece of lead, he says,
down into the sea, down down down until he thought he'd
never come up and suddenly he was all tangled in his half-open
parachute and he went crazy as a bat, as he tells it, and thought
the chute was an octopus that had him—like the octopus in
Hugo's story—and he fought it like mad and was losing the
fight too when suddenly a voice said, *Take it easy, boy.* A thousand times that voice had said it to him when he was a kid.

Once when he and his father were fishing and the boat had capsized in a squall; when he took his first high dive and his father stood there watching; when he had scarlet fever; when their car slid over a precipice and trembled on a big oak stump and then settled down and stayed there.

"He came to, realized he was fighting his chute, let go, and was up on top of the sea, got his raft open, crawled in and sent up a flare. Sat there waiting. Cold. Bleeding. And the voice kept saying *Take it easy.* 'And I knew the rest of it for his whole life said it: *You can't give in.*'

"Jim never told that story in camp. He'd laugh when they asked him what happened to him and say, 'Well, I had a little argument with an octopus about something that happened in the Middle Ages. He bit off my leg and I bit his off and that's about all there is to it.'

"Steve and Preacher and Professor—and Sammie. Sammie was a colored boy from Mississippi. His folks were renters on a cotton farm. Sammie is a graduate of Fisk. A great guy. Has a brilliant mind. Going to do research in chemistry when he gets out. Had the best collection of funny stories I've ever heard. Said they were his Dad's and Granddad's stories. Used to sing to us at night. He'd been one of the Fisk Singers in college. Now and then he'd sing things from *Mignon, La Bohème, La Figaro.* But what we liked were the old spirituals. Those arias couldn't talk to us in our trap. The spirituals came straight inside.

"I wonder if you can understand them until you hear them while you *are* trapped," he said. "Of course, everyone is in some kind of a trap, I guess—

"Well, anyway—Sammie would sing. And one night a guy

from Chicago said, 'You'd think you were still a slave, singing those damned old slave songs.'

"Nobody said a word for about five minutes. Then old Sam said, easy-like, 'Every man is a slave, bud, until he frees his mind and heart of shame and fear and hate. I'm not smart enough to know that. But my parents knew it. And I am beginning to believe it in this prison camp.'"

We shuffled words that night, laying them down between us, reshuffled again and again the old deck of human experience, laying down more words to look at. But we were not quite satisfied, either of us, with what we saw there: *courage* was a word we looked at a long time; and *risk*; *sacrifice* was another that we kept turning this way, that, knowing it has a profound meaning for the race of men. There was not a man in that prison camp who had not shown courage and who had not risked his life many times during the war. Even Hector. And, had any one of them died—even Hector—others would have spoken of his death as a "sacrifice" for his country. *Fortitude?* They had all slogged it out, those who lived through it. "You did—or you quit." But neither of us could find in those important words what the young paratrooper was seeking. *Responsibility* we looked at longer. "Yes," he said, "Steve felt that; and Jim, and Preacher, and Sammie; they acted as if what happened to us in that place was *their* concern. Something they were responsible for.

"Now isn't that an amazing thing when you come to think of it? And why did they?" and he smiled in the amused, puzzled and yet understanding way which I had grown used to and fond of, during the evening.

But there was one word neither of us thought of. And it seems strange that we did not. As the years passed, and again and again I went over in my mind what was said in that café (for I was impressed not so much by the incidents which any prisoner of war can match, but by the young man's need to get at the deeper meanings of the experience) I still could not find the word.

*Fortitude* I kept returning to, for it is one of the durable words of human experience, holding within it the essence of survival. "Muddling through," as the English understate it. "Slogging it out," Americans say. I thought again and again of Jim's father: "Take it easy, boy"—and the silent remainder of that sentence. I remembered, in John Hersey's *Hiroshima*—and nothing in the book is so moving—that great crowd huddled together in the park. It was the night after the bomb fell. There they were, wounded, burned, dying. Shocked beyond terror. And making not one sound. Just there. Breathing. Taking it. Not giving in. A little later, some would find reasons for living, but most would just keep living, that's all. If the breath of life could be held in them.

In prison and concentration camps all over the world, in disasters too big to be called one's personal ordeal, fresh meanings of that word have been found in recent years. But in every life there is a little of it. And a great deal in most lives. Lives of "quiet desperation" lived with quiet fortitude: next door to us, down the street, out in the shacks, on Park Avenue —wherever man has been reduced to the minimum of what is required to keep his spirit alive.

Something close to it we see in animal life and in plant life. There is a little dogwood tree on my ridge, planted in the wrong place, with too little moisture and too impoverished a soil and with too much sun and wind, but it has slogged it out for twenty years, growing only a few inches, never bearing a blossom. But it is still there, still alive. I would not dare say it has fortitude but deep in its life cells it has something that won't let go. And fortitude is, I think, the human spirit's equivalent of this.

But *fortitude* would not answer the question of what caused Steve and Preacher and Jim and Sammie to be what they were in that camp. There was another word and I kept searching. One day, I found it: *Honor*. It is a word of masculine gender for it has come largely out of man's experience, not woman's. The only word that matches its quality is *responsibility* which woman may claim, I think, as having first grown out of her long-time relationship with helpless infants and from her profound desire and need to safeguard human life within her own body and in the home. The two words had fused in four men's lives and brought forth a quality of experience whose ambience dimmed the monstrous, obscene events of that prison and pushed them to the edge of the mind. The important thing in all that loneliness and filth and cruelty and death was the fact that they could somehow find their way to a cleared place above the mess and disorder and pull the other men up there with them. They got on top of the experience by means of what responsibility and honor have meant not only to them but to centuries of men and women and they held most of the others there with them.

*Man's honor.* . . . It is a phrase one does not hear often, nowadays. Not many novels are written about it. Not many poems.

The masses have not learned, yet, how to pronounce it. When they do, they will no longer be "the masses" but will rise to the eminence of "the people."

*Honor* is a word that could, if believed in by enough people, completely destroy totalitarianism as it expresses itself in other countries and in our own. For it gives dignity and value to a man's personal and public relationships; it makes means as important as ends; it confers quality on experience. But the trouble is, it cannot live long under a communist or fascist regime—for how can it be cherished by the children who grow up there? Perhaps for a few years their parents may help them believe in it. But not for long. The pressures grow too severe; the old folks die out. The children hear less and less about the word. It is not in the newspapers; nor in books; nor on television. It acquires a quick archaism. Is no longer "correct." Dictators do all they can to keep it away from the young people for they loathe and fear it more than treason. Naturally. A traitor? Destroy him. A man with honor? You can kill him but his honor does not die. It lingers, like a nimbus, over the page of history and in the secret places of the people's hearts.

But, too often, honor has been a spiritual luxury which only the favored among men could afford. The impoverished of body and mind, beaten down through the centuries? How can honor grow in them when they have rarely known esteem or shared in the great adventures of mankind? Is it then an aristocratic virtue? No. Although it began to grow among a favored few, it grew there because they highly valued themselves as human beings, and it lives easily wherever men esteem themselves. It is, therefore, a virtue peculiarly well fitted for a democratic climate where all men are accepted and share its freedoms and responsibilities. More and more I find myself believing that you can gauge how much real quality there is in a country by the value its people put on their individual honor. It is a severe test. But freedom alone is not enough to give excellence to a people.

In fascist and communist countries, one does not see often, in public, either freedom or honor. It is *loyalty* the people wear —and they wear it where it will show. They are compelled to. It is the official mark of totalitarianism. As totalitarianism increases—in a school or a country or a church—the use of the word loyalty increases. A strange and frightening word. The mob's word. The gang's word. A word people shout in unison —while honor and responsibility and integrity are words only an individual can speak, and act out. *Loyalty* is not too evil a word, perhaps, when youngsters use it, in early adolescence, as they begin to identify clumsily, primitively, with their little gang or group (right or wrong). Not too bad—if they can only outgrow it as they outgrow their treble voices. But a dangerous word, too, and they should know its dangers and limitations. They should know it is only a mask that covers one's real relationship, or one's lack of a relationship. Loyal to somebody? But what is your real relationship with that person? Loyal to your government? But what is your real relationship? Does it have responsibility and honor in it?

Treason is a criminal act and can be dealt with reasonably as can other criminal acts. But feelings? How does one measure the quality of a man's relationship with a large entity such as church or school or government? It is an interesting fact, and one many of us have observed all our lives, that people demand loyalty of us only when they are doing something to us (or to somebody else) of which we don't approve and cannot whole-heartedly participate in, and which weakens our love and ad-miration. Let's admit it: *loyalty* is a verbal switch-blade used by little and big bosses to force us quickly to accept a questionable situation which our intelligence and conscience should reject.

I can easily imagine a fine prosperous growing country or school or home where the word *loyalty* is never used, nor the gesture required of anyone there; but I cannot imagine a home, a church, or school, or country that would have excellence in it were honor and responsibility not cherished by those who be-long to it. What would you have left?

Not much that can keep the quality of human relationships creative and good. Not much that can keep a man believing in his importance as a person. Not much that can help any of us come through an ordeal with more wisdom than when we en-tered it and with deepened resources of character.

Perhaps it is because I believe in "quality folks" that these two words have risen in my mind above all others as I seek my way to the heart of the meaning of ordeal in human experience. Quality folks: not "aristocracy," not "rich people," not the learned, not the white race, not people who happen to have ancestors who understood honor and accepted responsibility but people *who themselves* have learned the meaning of these words and the quality they give a man's relationships not only with other people but with himself.

Honor is not conferred by others but is something a man grows within himself. Its seed is in every ordeal he undergoes and in every relationship of his life and it flowers or dies ac-cording to how he comes through the ordeal and what he creates out of the relationship.

But to flower, it has first to be made fertile and only a sense of responsibility seems to have that power. Sammie, a researcher in chemistry from a Mississippi farm, understood this; and Jim, a Dartmouth professor who went to P.S. 116 in New York, and Steve who operates a filling station in a small town in California, and Preacher from Iowa. They understood that no man is alone in ordeal. There are others who care (the whole world cares) and one cannot dishonor these silent invisible relationships. One may not come through alive and the world may never know how one kept the faith but this faith with Man and his infinite possibilities must be kept.

To do so requires of a man or a woman a courage that often reaches the level of heroism. No one can live responsibly and with honor even in the smallest, quietest community without running great risks of losing something one cherishes. But courage, surely, is not what the one who has it seeks or values, in itself. It is a consequence of one's way of life, not a goal. Of course we love the word, and with a fervor that *fortitude* does not draw out of us—perhaps because *courage* concerns the individual while *fortitude* is a quality that the multitude has, also. But courage is a word for others to use about us, not something we can seek for ourselves. Like greatness and happiness and peace, courage comes and settles quietly within us while our mind and dreams are focussed elsewhere—it comes when we are trying not to let others down or our image of ourselves and the human race down, or our secret dream down. It comes to us as it has always come when we are living honorably and responsibly.

"But everybody cannot rise to the heights. Be realistic!"

It is true. Everyone cannot be like these four young men.

Nor can everyone rise to the greatness of a Michelangelo or a Mozart or a Beethoven, or Shakespeare or Li Po or Tagore, or Freud or Einstein or Gandhi or Eleanor Roosevelt or Albert Schweitzer. Everyone cannot measure up to the honor and responsibility felt by the young airplane hostess (in the newspaper headlines a year or so ago) who, about to leave the burning plane after her passengers were out, heard a mother from the safety of the ground call, "Get my baby!" and returned to those flames to try to save the baby whose mother had run out and forgot it. She perished in her attempt. But there are not many of us who would not prefer to be the dead little airplane hostess rather than the mother who forgot.

No, everyone is not talented enough, selfless enough, energetic, imaginative, intelligent, wise, or loving enough to have quality as a person. But the glory is that there are many who do. And they are the people who give life its patina. They are the singers and the poetry of this world.

And the rest of us? We can listen. We can relate ourselves to the singers and the poetry. Not only can we, we have a profound obligation to do so. For until a relationship is fused between the heroic deed and the rest of us, until a dialogue takes place between the great painting and those who look on it, the great book and those who read it, the act of sacrifice and those for whom it was made, it has not become itself. It has not yet found its quality of greatness.

In Malraux's *The Twilight of the Absolute* there are these lines which I think of often for they have important meaning for me:

"Genius imposes on the ages a language constantly modified, like an echo answering each successive age with its own voice, and what the masterpiece keeps up is not a monologue, however authoritative, but a dialogue triumphant over Time."

Art, as is true of all of man's profound experiences, is not for art's sake, nor for religion's sake, nor for the sake of beauty nor for any "cause." Art is for man's sake. It may be for one man's sake, or two billion. It may be for man today or man a hundred years from now. No matter. Man, the artist, creates what he creates *for himself as a living part of mankind*—not because of external compulsion but because of a passionate need to bring forth the inviolate part of his deepest experience and fuse it with elements of both earth and human past until it suddenly has a life of its own. And when he does this, other men call it theirs, also. The dialogue may rise and fall in cadence, now becoming a mighty chorus in which the whole world seems to be participating, now only a whisper. But it never ceases. A time will come when it seems to rise again from the dead: that piece of sculpture or an entire age of painting, or a book or poem—and once more, millions of men are talking with it, sharing their unborn dream with this ancient thing and taking from it what their dream needs to bring it alive.

And by the listening and the sharing we not only are enriched but we bestow wealth on our world. For we are "in dialogue," we are forming a new quality of human relationship. In doing so, we are, as Henry Miller has said, "underwriting" our age "with our lives," because we believe utterly in its power to transmute its terror and grief and sorrow and mistakes into a music which the future can claim as its own.

And yet, how alone the artist feels in his ordeal. As alone as Guillaumet when his plane came down in the Andes; as Saint Exupéry on that flight to Arras when he came to terms with the word *responsibility*; or the young Lindbergh as he opened up a new path in the sky. As alone as little Bill on those nights when his heroes somehow were not there to sustain him and it was too dark to read the letters his father had written him in Korea; or Marty, as she struggled to find her way to the love in her nature which was so long blocked off by her fears; or Mrs. Timberlake, arranging shells and starfish on small windswept graves to speak her faith; or two Negro women, on a stormy night, driving along a dark highway—who must have felt that the whole world had a white face and there was no acceptance written on it.

But the artist is never alone. He has an intimate relationship with the wood he is carving, the paint and canvas, the words, the stone: these are making their demands and their plea and offering their gifts and he is answering and the dialogue sustains him—as do another man's beliefs and memories and the knowledge that there are those who care. The artist knows something else, wordless, oftentimes, but he knows it deep within him: that were it not for the struggle and the loneliness he undergoes in his search for integrity there would be no strength or beauty in his work. (And though art is not for the sake of beauty, beauty must be there or the profound revelation the artist makes would be unbearable.)

The artist in us knows, the poet in us knows: it is the mark not of ordeal but of mastered ordeal that gives a face, a life, a great event, or a great work of art its style. The wound is there but the triumph also, the death and the birth, the pain and the deep satisfactions: it is all there in delicate equilibrium, speaking to us.

# ～ 15 ～

AND now, I must close my book although the journey has not ended. It will never end. I have only begun to see what it is all about: this stay of man's on earth. Its meaning begins to come clear, here, there, and quickly is covered up again by heavier mists rolling in from the unknown. Mists that are blowing away every day, gathering again, clearing, once more gathering. And yet, though it seems to be a view dimmed with thick immovable uncertainties, I know—we all know—that slowly, gradually, with limited but increasing certitude we are learning more about our world and ourselves.

We are so young, they tell us: only a quarter of a million years has man, as *homo sapiens*, been here. Life on this earth in other forms has been going along with enormous energy for perhaps two billion years and there is no reason to believe that it will not continue for another two billion. But we are new-comers. And we are different. Soft-bodied and soft-skinned and soft-hearted and hard-headed; with a terrible vulnerableness and an utterly miraculous gift for taking it easy and not giving in and somehow coming through. Not an "improved" species of animal life in the old-fashioned sense of evolution is this

creature. No. The word is *different*. Different because we speak
and we love, because we yearn for knowledge and long to be
tied to other human beings. Different because we would rather
die than be deprived of tenderness and truth—and would die,
were we permanently cut off from them. Because we are painfully aware of our separation from all we want to be bound to
that is close to us and dimly aware of our distance from God.
Because we know brokenness, and cut by its sharp edge, can
feel the meaning of wholeness. Because we have learned to
gather up our experience and store it safely so others can use
and keep using it; keep using an event ten thousand years after
it happened, turning it, feeling it, staring at it, suddenly identifying with one or another aspect of it; keep dreaming about a
painting, a statue, a poem, a symphony, turning it, feeling it,
suddenly drawing part of it into one's self and claiming it as
one's own; keep thinking about a man who died for his beliefs,
keep remembering, until suddenly one day we, too, understand
why a man must risk his life and all he loves for something he
believes in even though he cannot prove that it is true. He must
do it, sometimes; and though history and science may prove
the belief is wrong they can never prove the man who died was
wrong to risk his life. For risk is necessary to life—and there is
no greatness in life without great risk. Our little security systems are not to eliminate the risk but to help us ride it out as a
seaworthy boat rides a storm out.

Now a new irony—or perhaps a very old one—makes its
entrance. As the walls that threatened to smother us are falling,
as distance and ignorance which once we feared and dreaded
now crumble—and we are given, for the first time in history, a
nearness to each other and to knowledge that no one thought

possible until a few decades ago—we grow afraid. That is understatement. We are terrorized so completely, at times, that the intelligence we have depended on for thousands of years seems to have turned to stone inside us. This new ordeal of proximity to each other and to scientific facts which even the finest minds among us can scarcely comprehend the significance of, arouses in us archaic insecurities—and suddenly new forms of a very old anxiety are released upon the world.

The ordeal of isolation and ignorance and poverty was hard enough to bear. But we learned to take it, somehow; and developed within us resources of faith and fortitude, of humor and art and ritual and play and work and a handsome vocabulary, and armor-like defenses which shut out from sight, ear and mind—and even from the heart—what we could not deal with. These were honorable and effective weapons for the times in which they were developed and some of them we shall never, wisely, abandon. The human race achieved incredible expertness in their use; amazing when one considers that we learned: to shut out completely what was plainly seen and yet could not be faced up to; to act out in ritual and ceremonials deep truths our tongues feared to speak of; to call it "wrong to know" what could not be found out anyway even though we desperately needed to know it; to maintain silence and secrecy about ourselves when the tongue wanted to sing (or scream, perhaps) its story aloud; to transcend with belief what would otherwise have crushed the spirit out of a man, and to endure with scarcely a groan, and often with magnificent laughter and wit, what could not be eased or avoided.

Then came the new: the ordeal of sudden closeness to the strange person and the strange fact; the ordeal of sudden realization that what we thought was "fate" or "God's Will" need not be; the ordeal of things, things crowding life, soft velvety things, and hard things like machines and gadgets; and strangest experience of all, the ordeal of an abrupt view of our own childhood, given us when science swung wide the doors of the nursery and insisted that we look in—which, with the quick plunge into man's past and the earth's past, took away from us forever the naive absolute which we used to hold to, substituting a relativism too easily translated by the sophisticated and the glib into a way of life which held no values in it.

It was too much. There we were: stripped of ignorance and isolation (both of which had finally become dear to us); compelled to look at great machines that threaten to roll over their creator as if he were a fly; compelled to look at our naked absurd uncivilized and much too powerful babyhood; compelled to accept the vast unknown power of the Unconscious within us at the same time that we were trying to accept the staggering idea that life had been on this earth two billion years and man had not even been here, until a moment ago.

Blow followed blow in rapid succession until the human ego was hardly more than pulp. Then science (or should we say the step-and-fetch-its of science?) knocked out that durable old ego which had seen man through some pretty tough spots by a shattering attack on his belief, gained slowly, painfully, that he is important to God and important to God's plan for this evolving universe. In different words, and expressed in different ceremonials, human beings had believed this a long time and the belief had given them their manhood and womanhood and their deep abiding sense of honor and responsibility for their fellow men.

The bells began to strike. And man's ego lay there. It looked for a little while as if it was done for. But not for long. It rose, dizzy and waving, but it rose again and brought man up to his feet also. That is the wonder of it.

He could not look steadily but he looked science in the face and he was no longer terrified by what he saw there. Still a little anxious—he will always be, and should be—but the terror began to leave him. He began to remember a few things: he knew he had not been on this earth long, compared to the 50,000,000 years the ant has lived here but no ant could paint Mona Lisa, or carve out the David, or write Beethoven's Seventh Symphony, or build the George Washington bridge, or invent the airplane or discover penicillin or dream up and organize the United Nations, or become a great surgeon or create a great industry or think up something as new and as effective as a labor union or—

He began to come to his senses.

He began to see childhood not as a room with no exit (as he had first misinterpreted the knowledge Freud and others gave to the world) but as a room with ten thousand doors and windows which can be opened from outside and inside and which lead to good and bad destinations. He began to believe that one can return for what one needs without being imprisoned there. He began to understand that the only power that can lock it into a tight place is the fear that silence and mystery and guilt breed. He began to find it possible to accept the place not as hell's kitchen where sins are brewed but, matter of factly, as the nursery it has been and always will be where the little human animal learns to feel like a human being and to grow into one; where he learns to value love and tenderness and knowledge if it is fed him and to protest if he is deprived of these necessities; where he learns to accept frustration "like a little man" if it has meaning for him but where he refuses (as he should) to accept a meaningless world and raises all manner of disturbance if the powers around him (limited quite possibly to parents) put him in chains simply because they can. He sees childhood as the seed-bed it is; but he knows what happens there is not the last chance a child has. It is only his first: all his life, every time he goes through a crisis either of growth or accident or outward change in his world he has another chance, another opportunity to clear up the unfinished business of childhood, of adolescence, of young manhood, of senescence—

He began to see memory as not always a threatening mess of crumpled geometry and limp watches and thighbones, but also as a boundless source of joy and pleasure, and a mighty defense against fear; for it has power to lift the pressure off, somehow —as it did for Marty one cold spring morning when a soft rain fell; as it did for the young paratrooper when his chute was slow in opening; as it did for Jim when he fought his "octopus"; as it has done for most of us in bleak and terrible moments.

Things began to clear, a little. And for all of us. We are beginning to see *home* not only as the place where hate and guilt and obscene fantasies and the ills we call "mental" and "criminal" begin but where our love and knowledge and sense of responsibility begin, also. Not only as the place where tyranny has its first big chance at a child but where good will has *its* first chance, too. Not only as a befouled nest but as a secure haven to which we can return now and then, if only in memory, when we sorely need reassurance and peace.

And the "Oedipus complex?" Why was it hard for us to acknowledge the reality of an experience common to all children? Perhaps the difficulty lay not so much in the fact as in the way the fact was brought to our attention. Sigmund Freud was not only a wise and honest and great scientist, he was a dramatic poet. It was not what he told us that sent us into panic —the actual content of his scientific findings (which we already knew dimly) we are durable enough to take. It was this scientist's spectacular use of language. Had Shakespeare laid on a baby's mind and body the weight of so grand and tragic a metaphor as the "Oedipus complex" we might have responded to it with a smile. After all, we'd say, he is partly right, and too, he doesn't really know. But the metaphor loaded with the authority of science was more than we honestly felt the baby (or his parents) could bear. I don't know how "honest" we were, actually; in panic, people's minds become pickpockets and sneak thieves. But we—even those of us who deeply respect and admire Sigmund Freud as the great germinal thinker he was—felt a stubborn resistance that originated in part, of course, from not liking to be confronted with the inescapable facts of the immense power parents have over helpless children, the immense power our buried past has over us, and the immense power a weak infant's feelings may have over tomorrow's history page. It was all this, but more. It was the way Freud, with one metaphor, pushed the diapered baby onto a stage where only Greek heroes feel at home, turned the lights on, tuned up the Chorus, and insisted that we look at what we saw there and accept it as the literal truth about sucklings and their first tremulous attempt at finding new ties to bind them to this lonely, difficult, complicated and utterly beguiling world they are compelled to call "home."

(Perhaps there is, after all, a therapeutic if not esthetic justification for the use of jargon in the social and medical sciences. Maybe it is the only way to reduce the shock of new knowledge about ourselves. By the time a few writers understand it well enough to translate it into the language of common experience it has lost its surprise quality and the public is prepared to take it—in small doses.)

But even with the weight of his authority, had Freud told us, in language less tragic and fateful and nearer perhaps to Carson McCuller's tender, humorous and perceptive words, that every child wants passionately to be "a member of the wedding," we should have assented with an "of course." We know it is true. We know it, just as we know that every child wants, now and then, to be a member of the funeral, too. Because the child wants to belong: yearns to be a part of the great ceremonials of human experience, yearns to be both the bride and the groom; yearns to feel one with the mother and simultaneously one with the father and one with its self; longs to be lover and enemy, to be the mourner and the one mourned for, to be the slave and the master, the sinner and the judge, seeking ties and roles, a thousand new ones, possible and impossible, to restore a little of the old security and satisfactions of its prenatal life.

Learning that some of the ties he wants to make and some of the roles he wants to play are impossible is his first moral ordeal, and acceptance of this hard bleak reality sometimes gives to a three-year-old's face a poignant valor so delicately fused of resignation and rebellion that it has the validity of a great master's drawing.

How powerful words are in building up and breaking down the walls in our minds. If they have new truth in them, they do both. Sigmund Freud's words shocked my generation into confused and, retrospectively, laughable states of mind. We played dead, we made poor jokes, or became abject disciples, or got angry and sneered at greatness. But his words broke the awful silence. They tore the mystery out of a place where it should never have been and stirred up enough energy for us to move the debris so that our sense of decency and good will and love and mercy could begin housecleaning the nursery and our own musty memories—washing away the mess of fear and false guilt and terrifying silence that had left a heavy stench of uncleanliness there. And his words wrote, I think, the first shadowy draft of the child's Bill of Rights as a human being.

These were traumatic experiences we underwent. Image and image ideal were broken and mended, lost forever sometimes, recreated now and then in the intense heat of changes taking place in man's way of thinking and talking about himself.

But the difficulty was exacerbated by the fact that neither scientists nor we had enough humility. They were reluctant to give up their new real power, and we were as reluctant to give up the old fictitious power which ignorance and silence made us feel we had over our lives. Neither wanted to assume the new obligations of the new ordeal. We did not want to learn the new truths about ourselves; and they did not want to bend their fine new science in service to human life.

It was a holy war—for God was used by both opponents—fought bitterly with ourselves and with each other, for and against knowledge and ignorance, for and against power and humility. "If you are for science," some said, "then you are against God. For we have had God a long time and ignorance a long time; hence, God and ignorance are one and the same." And a few scientists behaved almost as foolishly, for they said, "Now science can eliminate ignorance. As for God? We cannot prove He exists. Therefore, theoretically at least, He does not exist until we prove He does. And, anyway, with such knowledge and power as man now has, why does he need God?"

And so, many "gave up God" and "accepted science." They became "rational," they talked about a mechanistic universe, they smiled at values, snickered at ideals. They were "realists." Prayer became obsolete. "Why pray, when science can cure you? Ten dollars worth of penicillin for pneumonia is worth a dozen prayers." It seemed not to occur to them that prayer might mean something more than shaking a tin cup in God's face: That it could be an attempt to relate ourselves to the unknown potentialities for good within us; to bind ourselves humbly to something bigger than we are; to probe more deeply into the significance of man's role in this universe; to catch a glimpse of the wonder and mystery and love and hope that the word *God* holds within it. No. Science was our new "servant" now; and God was no longer needed. He could retire to our backyard past and abide with the "primitives."

And all the time, the great men of science, Einstein, Eddington, Jeans, many others, were trying to tell us, as Einstein has said so movingly:

"The most beautiful and most profound emotion we can experience is the sensation of the mystical. It is the sower of all true science. He to whom this emotion is a stranger, who can no longer wonder and stand rapt in awe, is as good as dead. To know that what is impenetrable to us really exists, manifesting itself as the highest wisdom and the most radiant beauty which our dull faculties can comprehend only in their most primitive forms—this knowledge, this feeling is at the center of true religiousness."*

But men—those for and against—were angry and frightened and confused and would not listen.

Those "against science," while using applied science every day of their lives, held on to their ignorance as stubbornly as they held on to God. In a most interesting and completely human way, God and ignorance are twisted together, even now, in millions of people's minds and feelings. Many sincerely do not want to "give up" God. But there is something in that ignorance which they don't want to give up, either. It is, I think, a spurious sense of goodness. If only we can keep ourselves ignorant enough we can worship God and feel good while doing harm to others and to ourselves. This way, sanctity can be purchased at cut rates. And we have always loved a bargain, especially when we cheat ourselves. The ego learns this early, and is marvelously adept at using ignorance as a shield to protect us from the impact of our ideals.

There are numerous uses for ignorance and man knows them all for he has lived with it so long. Most seductive is the knowledge that if we can keep others ignorant we can more easily maintain our power over them. Parents learned this long before dictators and demagogues guessed it. The church learned it

* Lincoln Barnett, *The Universe and Dr. Einstein* (New York: William Sloane Associates, 1948).

before communists and fascists knew their ABC's. And there were many groups, often antagonistic to each other, who felt their power imperiled by the enlightenment which science would inevitably effect, and promptly threw their weight on the side of "ignorance and God."

The confusion grew—as it always does in holy wars. Actually, men were fighting, as they fight in every generation, the ancient battle within themselves between power and humility.

But we are beginning to understand. Beginning to know that we need both science and God: for both the known and the as-yet-unknown are and will always be in our lives. We can no more decide "for" one and "against" the other than we can decide we are "for" the past and "against" the future. As is true in most wars, the surface conflict was a false one. The fighting words tried but did not succeed in shattering a great and indivisible whole.

It has always been a difficult and complex struggle: this bringing humility and power into a harmonic relationship within ourselves. Each change forces us to make a new fusion. Power is lost by one part of our natures, gained by another— just as in the world's affairs one group loses, another gains. And humility, too often, is lost by both for conflict stiffens one's belief that one can do no wrong and there is nothing one does not know. The Absolute gets easily in control.

And it seems to be in control of men's minds, today: there is so much power in the hands of ruthless men and so much of arrogance and defensiveness in their words that it is difficult to believe humility is left in any of us. But underneath the sound and fury, there is increasing among men and women across the earth a willingness to use their powers for the sake of others, to change their personal security systems, even to admit mistakes if by doing so, someone else can be helped. It is strange that the enduring events of human experience—those for which an age becomes known in history—seem always to happen quietly. Perhaps it is because they first happen inside one man, or one woman, inside another, another: moving quietly, moving swiftly sometimes, until a new thing has happened in the world, a trend of such amplitude and importance is established that old pathways trod for generations are abandoned. Aching questions, unanswered, are simply erased from the mind for they no longer matter.

This new humility—not yet felt by dictators and demagogues and many others in public affairs—is giving the world a new strength and a new harmony.

I have seen it on this journey.

There was a morning when I heard a mother say, as I slipped in and sat down with the group:

"That moment, I saw it: I was demanding of my child that he be normal, like a little animal. But the very fact of his being human makes it impossible for him to fit a 'normal' pattern. I saw this. I did not think it in these words, then; I couldn't. It was later—after I had read and studied and tried to learn more about it all—that I found words for it. One day, in a book titled *Evolution in Action*, by Julian Huxley, I read these words:

> 'Man's individual development . . . continues through-
> out his life, and it can take place in all sorts of direc-
> tions; while in animals there is only one normal

> pattern to be realized. . . . Animal types have limited
> possibilities, and sooner or later exhaust them: man has
> an unlimited field of possibilities, and he can never
> realize all of them.'

They opened the door for me. Perhaps this eminent biologist
would be surprised to know that a handful of his words could
bring to a woman with a retarded child the answer she had
sought for months. But they were the words I needed to hear.

"But this day when I changed, I was feeling—not thinking.
I had been ashamed so long. I had wished, for months, that he
was dead. I did not say so. I cheated. I said, 'If God would
only take him.' "

A quick smile passed from face to face of the mothers
listening.

"It was an experience I wanted to cut myself loose from and
forget. Look at all my friends, I'd say to myself: what *they*
have brought forth. Then look at what—

"You see, I missed the whole point: Bearing a child, carrying
it around in our bodies, that is not motherhood. We are only
the instruments of life during that part of the process. Of
course our bodies and feelings play a positive role then, but it
is happening on a deep level beyond our conscious control—
most of it. But afterward, then motherhood begins. The real
job. And there I was, mourning my failure as a mother because
of an accident of genes and chromosomes and chemistry and
all the rest of it about which science still knows so little. The
prologue is written out by ten thousand ancestors—mine and
my husband's—and my own metabolism, maybe, and the hundred possible accidents, like viruses—so much we don't know

yet—that can occur during those nine months a child is growing. But when *my* scene opened—well, I am afraid I did not
know the rudimentary meaning of being a mother."

"They call us rejecting mothers," another spoke suddenly.
"I suppose they are right. In a way. But I rebel when I hear
people who have not been through it put this experience in a
capsule and drop it in a box with other little capsules and
stamp on the box *Maternal Rejection*."

"But if *we* are only beginning to understand the meaning of
those words *rejection* and *acceptance*—how they are wrapped
up with every feeling we have ever had about ourselves—we
can hardly expect them to know what it is all about. Then too,
it makes them feel morally superior—and don't you remember
how wonderful it once was to feel *superior*?"

The laughter among the mothers was bright and brittle.

"It does not matter what we are, or what they say—if we
only change," the first mother was again speaking. "That is
why I said my story is not a sad one. Because one day, I saw
what I was doing. I was preparing dinner that evening, and
my little son was sitting there on the floor, lumpily playing
with his toys. And I looked at him, trying to keep the tears
back. And he looked up and smiled at me, as if to say, *We'll
make it, Mommie*. It happened then. He loves me, I thought
suddenly. And I knew I loved him, too, and couldn't let him
down.

"We signed a pact with each other that day. Once you do
that, the rest of it is easy. Because it becomes a challenge to
you on every level of your life. Your brain, heart, values, your
imagination, sense of humor—everything gets involved as you
begin to help your son find *his* life, different from the others,

but *his*. It becomes exciting and you like doing it. There is no more conflict inside.

"Up to this time, I had never talked about real things to anyone. Not even to myself. I had a patter that was gay and seemed to entertain everybody no end. Why talk about real things when you can get by so easily?

"In all my life, I had not known humility. I was easily humiliated. But humility? No."

"Nor I," said another woman sitting in that circle of mothers. "I hated psychology. To admit I could make mistakes? Impossible. I covered up. All my life I hid everything—the Soviet Union has never had a curtain as thick as mine. And then, my little girl came. I wanted to hide her, too, but my husband accepted her from the beginning. 'She is so sweet,' he would say. And I hated him for saying it. Again and again he said it, and his face looked as if he meant it. He'd say, 'She is just different; and that means we shall have to find a different way to teach her. There are ten thousand possibilities.' You see, he understood motherhood better than I did."

"Why not call it fatherhood?" said a tall gray-haired woman. "Being a good father doesn't end with contributing a few sperms to the project. Or does it?"

There was more laughter. This time, clear and rippling.

"My husband dislikes our child," said another. "And that is a part of our difficulty. He thinks these talks are morbid. 'Where is it going to get *you*, or *me*?' he says."

"But he is so wrong, if you will forgive my frankness," said a pretty girl who looked almost too young to be a mother. "Coming here has given me immense hope. I can't tell you what it means to be able to talk with others who understand.

It becomes unbearable—people's pity. 'That poor girl,' they say. And you want to give up. It doesn't help a bit."

No, it doesn't help, for pity has no hands and cannot come close enough.

Now they had begun to share with each other their new ways of teaching. They were talking shop: ingenious ideas, amazing things they had stumbled on. They were laughing, explaining, teasing each other. The young pretty thing was saying, "You should have seen Jackie yesterday! He has learned to wash his hands. He went to the washbowl and *did it*! I was as proud as if he had walked out of Harvard with *summa cum laude*."

I slipped away. A week before, I had been with mothers whose children are blind. They were searching for their own and their children's possibilities, making the most of what was left. Another day, the group was composed of those whose children have speech difficulties.

Mothers, talking together. Other groups—Alcoholics Anonymous, parents whose children were not in step with the family rhythms—sharing experiences, trying to find the constructive way. Confessing. Not because a tyrant had demanded a confession from them. No. This is a new kind of confession: people coming together to talk about meaningful experiences, laying down their spurious goodness and sham omniscience, sharing sorrow and success in order to help others, and themselves.

Long ago, St. Augustine wrote his *Confessions*; in loneliness, trying to bind the secret part of his nature to God and his world. Not often, since, has anyone written with so much candor and grace. But scarcely a century has passed in the Western world that a man, a woman, has not tried to talk of love, and lust, and delight and anguish, and of feelings about God, seeking words for shadowy wordless relationships; sometimes as show-offs, but more often, I think, aching with the need to bring out and look at their own secret pain and joy. Heloise . . . Chaucer . . . Dante . . . now and then a saint . . . in memoir, legend, poetry they have felt compelled to tell the human story.

But after the Renaissance the silence thickened. Bleak need and desire and false ideas and no real knowledge of body and mind and disease and disaster brought rough weather to the heart of man. We were in agonized conflict about soul, body, and our tenderest relationships, and God; and silence seemed the only reliable defense against anxiety.

It is a strange and fascinating and involved story which has not yet been set down by historians: this emotional mutism which silenced men just as their hands were learning to write and the people were learning to read, and books were being printed; and worsened during those centuries when they began to declare their dignity and their rights, especially their right to freedom of speech and belief. As the silence increased, the dirty joke flourished and a large unwashed vocabulary, driven out of dictionaries, went underground and began to live a riotous life there, consorting with outlawed fantasies. . . . Wanting to be angels, we lived a way of life that bred many a monster, half-animal half-machine.

Of course there were dramatists who spoke gaily and sometimes bawdily in defiance of the prudery; and poets, and artists who felt no shame (and sometimes little responsibility). And Shakespeare with his delighted acceptance of life's farce and tragedy, roguery and foolery and wonder and tenderness spoke as no other tongue before or since: gathering up all of human experience and embracing it in his imagination, burnishing the image of man to a brightness that nothing has ever been able to dim. But the multitude forgot or never heard of him and the puritans banned him and the lesser playwrights, and, more and more completely, men and women rejected themselves, tearing off in guilt and shame and ignorance their most human and endearing qualities.

But even during the eighteenth, nineteenth and early twentieth centuries when the silence attained a kind of grandeur, so massive and unwieldy and official it had become, now and then a man did speak either in memoir or novel (a disguise writers and readers of these late centuries discovered to be most useful) of himself and others as he knew them to be: Stendhal, and that half-wise, half-foolish Rousseau, and De Quincey, and Samuel Butler; Dostoevsky, Rilke, Proust, Joyce, Havelock Ellis, Gide. And by the close of the nineteenth century Freud and his fellow scientists were publicizing their proofs of what the wise ones had long ago intuitively guessed.

Then came the injured ones: those who quietly told what it means to be blind, deaf, paralyzed, different in body or mind or in color: Helen Keller and her good teacher, Anne Sullivan; and Clifford Beers; and James Weldon Johnson. Then Marguerite Fischel set down in a book the story of her two cerebral palsied children and what she did to help the one who lived have a life, not like Carl's in my hometown, but a good, rich human life. Her son went to college, skated, rode horseback, lived actively and purposefully. As far as I know, Mrs. Fischel's was the first book written by a mother about these children, so long hidden away. Then Dr. Earl Carlson wrote his life story; later Pearl Buck wrote about her child "who never grew." The silence was gone. More and more individuals began to tell stories which, until then, people could not have whispered even to themselves: speaking of hurt bodies and hurt minds and hurt relationships, of mistakes and triumphs, proudly and with deep humility.

All these: St. Augustine . . . Rousseau . . . Stendhal . . . the great teachers like Comenius and Pestalozzi and Anne Sullivan . . Helen Keller . . . Freud . . . Havelock Ellis . . . the hurt ones . . . the mothers—all these opened the way. Finally, it was no longer a few lonely and brave individuals telling the world what it felt like, but groups of people, coming together not because they felt superior to others, or to fight others, or in snobbish withdrawal but to help others and in the doing of it, of course the miracle happened: they helped themselves.

It has crept upon us so quietly. We have hardly noticed. But it is one of the significant events of the twentieth century: these groups of men and women, finding their tongues, sloughing off the old mutism and doing it just as science gives them the means of world-wide communication. Not arguing, not debating, not defending and entrenching their past mistakes. Not on trial. Simply saying, "It was this way with me." We speak often of the great age of communication but radio and television have not yet explored the dramatic possibilities of conversations between those who have the humility and grace and insight and words to tell a truth about themselves that has profound meaning for others.

The importance of breaking the silence lies in our willingness to give up pretensions to a power and perfection we had no right to in the first place. In surrendering pretensions—which means abandoning old and beloved defenses—there is real pain. It is not easy. But those who have done so are finding and donating to the world a fresh strength and a new subtle quality of communication which come because they are in touch with others on the deepest levels of experience.

We are so used to contactless association in our modern life that it almost seems the only way to behave. But there is not only psychological but moral danger in activities that are de-humanized. For the core of morality lies in the realness of our relationships and identifications, the quality, the tenderness and truth they hold. Miss Molly, the good teacher; Marty and John, the good parents; Steve, Preacher, Sammie and Jim, Bud and Henry, the good friends; the good Little Grandma; Timothy, the good stranger; Bill's good surgeon: there is no substitute for the good human being in human affairs. No power, whether of science, wealth, guns or authority can take the place of real relationships.

We are learning this now—as parents and teachers and plain people.

The scientists are learning, too, that science becomes good only in service to human life.

I saw this happening, not long ago, in a dramatic way. It was at Toots Shor's. Late one winter afternoon. A party. In the room were men known across the earth for their distinguished medical achievements. There were philanthropists, psychia-trists, a writer or two, therapists, psychologists. A beautiful girl whose back had been broken in an automobile accident leaned slightly on her cane as she talked to a friend. There was a man in a wheelchair. A pleasant-faced woman, his wife, sat near him. Waiters were moving in and out. Toots Shor was near the doorway, beaming, watchful.

We had come to see the première of a documentary film made by Victor Solow and called *A New Beginning*. The story was of a paralyzed miner's rugged trip back to active life. The man, whose experience it was, sat quietly in his wheelchair waiting to take a second look at his own life. Man, watching himself. . . . We always try to remember, always paint a portrait of our experiences, distorting them, shaping, reducing, enlarging, giving them strange sharp colors or sometimes doing them in monochromes. But here a man's experience was documented on a film. What will this new potential do to the human memory, I thought, as I sat there waiting in the darkened room for the film to begin. Suppose parents were to document theirs and their child's experiences; suppose they set them down in film to look at, and talk over together, later; suppose this happened in many homes—what effect would it have on childhood, on human awareness, on memory?

The film began. Clean, swift camera work caught a mining town at dawn. Men with lunch kits going to work. Women sweeping front porches; opening windows. Sharp lines of house, roof, street. Men, more and more men going to work, down the street; down another street; another. A lyricism crept into the flow of images, as if the cameraman knew now that he was telling the world's story of men, working. The coal mine. The shaft. Men going down, down. The sudden accident. The slow return home on a stretcher. The long wait in bed. Lying there, finished. It used to be the last weary chapter. It was not this man's last chapter. After a stretch of months, he was taken to a rehabilitation hospital. There he began the struggle back. Learning to move an inch; another; sweating it out. And we, in Toots Shor's restaurant, watched him as he picked up his inner resources, one by one, trying this one, that, to help him find a way out of the trap. And finally he got out. He can move, walk, use his hands. He has a job. He has married.

But he could not have done it alone. There are disasters no man, however determined and brave, can come out of without others to help. To get this man back on his feet and into a job required knowledge that is the result of centuries of patient scientific research. It required the pooled skills of orthopedic surgeons, psychiatrists, occupational and physical therapists, psychologists; required the use of instruments invented in the fields of electronics, electricity, X-ray, metallurgy; required discoveries in chemistry, physics—

Even this could not have done it. The science and the instruments, and the new metals and plastics, and the antibiotics would not have put this man on his feet, had not someone believed it possible for a paralyzed man to walk and cared enough to find the means by which it could be done.

But it was more than this. Someone had, also, to possess the imagination to see that a surgeon has not completed his job when he does a skillful amputation, or puts a steel pin in a hip, or operates on a spine. He is—as I have heard that great orthopedic surgeon, Dr. Henry Kessler, say—operating not on a bone but on a life. "You cannot separate a man's body from his life." When he goes under anesthesia, his life goes under, too; and all his relationships; his job, his image of himself, his dreams. And when his body heals, if his life has not healed, if he is not back in the world, working, playing, dreaming again, relating himself—"well, we haven't finished our job, that is all."

In that dim room watching the film, was Dr. Howard Rusk. Much of its story had been made at the New York Institute of Physical Medicine and Rehabilitation, of which he is the director. During the Second World War, he, too, saw this mid-century vision: a man's life cannot be broken into fragments and these fragments of body, mind, emotions, skills treated as if they have no relation to each other or to the rest of him or to his family. Science has to think of man set in the center of his life, in the center of his past and future, related to those he loves, to his job, his hopes, pleasures, childhood, dreams, values and related also to the rest of us. There is no right way for science but to use its knowledge for man's whole life. And no right way for men but to accept, in humility, the help that can come only from the knowledge and good will of other men.

It is a just thing that man's body gave him the first patterns for his tools and machines, and now, in return, these tools and machines are giving him a new image of himself and helping him connect up with capacities he did not know he possessed. Instruments thought up by his brain, giving him a view of that brain which eyes, alone, could not see. Electricity, measuring for him his electrical rhythms. Electronics, radar, X-rays, radium, isotopes giving him new means by which to perceive himself and his world.

It is a wondrous thing, too, that speech long ago gave him a giant-size capacity for remembering and storing his experience and in doing so helped him explore the universe; and now, with the knowledge he found there and the humility he has presently found within himself, speech is once more helping him explore that memory and make the return trip to a childhood he was too young to understand when he left it.

A strange and lovely thing it is, too, that we are learning to accept the body's vast potentialities by learning to accept its brokenness and differences; and in finding ways to bind the fragments into a whole life we are finding a common ground where people of the earth can meet in understanding and sympathy.

And even as we accept *relativity* as a word that has a validity for our modern world which the *absolute* no longer has, we begin to understand that the word applies neither to God nor to human values. Morality is not relative; it is a *growing* concept that has sprung from the seed of the human being's need of others and his need to believe in God in order to keep the future open. It has grown as a tree grows, dropping its "moralities" as leaves fall; greening again. The leafing and the fall of the leaves cannot be confused with the steady growth of the tree itself, as men become more and more reverent of life, more and more aware of the power of love and tenderness in human affairs, more and more sure of their interdependence and their need for a wisdom which is not science but takes to itself all that science can contribute; more and more accepting of themselves as growing creatures who change as long as they live. We begin to understand that we can never have absolute knowledge of God and yet He is not "relative." It is simply that our knowledge is incomplete and while it will increase as we grow, always there will be the impenetrable between man and God.

It is coming together, now, into a whole: the dream and the means to implement the dream. Ever since men have felt tenderness and a love of the truth they have dreamed of a good life; a good way: what the Chinese philosophers called *Tao*; what Jesus called the Abundant Life; what Buddha spoke of as moral growth, as freedom from fear, as taking thought.

But it was impossible to attain. Tenderness and love of truth are not enough: there must be knowledge; there must be the means, the technics, the instruments by which disease can be cured, disasters avoided, ordeals survived, poverty and ignorance eradicated; there must be those who care enough to have the imagination to believe something can be done about it.

Now, for the first time, we are beginning to bring together the fragments: to bind childhood to the rest of our life so that our reason can control it and thus reduce the anxiety which dictators, inside and outside us, exploit so lushly; to tie body to mind to feelings to fantasies to belief; to relate these to the rest of mankind and to the world; to relate power to humility, and responsibility to honor and freedom; to keep tenderness and truth close together.

As I sat there watching that miner make his comeback, watching as numberless friends helped him (some of whom have been dead for centuries but whose knowledge is still here for him to use) I saw this: the symphonic fullness of life as it is possible for us to live it today. Man, directing; man, playing his instruments: one, ten thousand, two billion bodies and hands and minds and hearts bringing the dream into reality as dissonances build toward climax, resolve, mount again, resolve, mount again, held in key by belief, modulating into richer beliefs—making fabulous music.

It is man's role in this evolving universe (as Auden, Shelley, Tagore, and other poets have reminded us) to teach the terrors of his nature and his world to sing, to bring order out of chaos, to create the new from the debris of the old. And he is beginning, today, to have spectacular success in doing so.

A century from now, men may think it strange that we so long spoke of our times as the age of anxiety; that we let the greed of ordinary men and the power-lust of dictators and demagogues get out of bounds even for a brief span of years; for parallel with the anxiety and the terror and the inquisitors and exploiters and the awful poverty and ignorance there is another way of life building firmly, steadily, swiftly on scientific facts and technics and on men's newly discovered humility and dignity and on their concern for each other.

There has, of course, always been more love than hate in the world—else the human race would have died out long ago. But never in the world's history has there been so much tenderness and understanding shown children, as today. Never so much concern for the welfare of the stranger and for those who are different. Never such willingness to lay aside spurious goodness and omniscience. And for the first time, we have the means to implement the good feelings, the honesty, the insight; the means of instant world-wide communication, the means of quick getting together, the means of recreating a storm-ruined town almost overnight; of eliminating poverty; of healing not only a body but a whole life.

No, our age will never go down in history as the age of anxiety, nor as the atomic age. It will be stamped with the mark of a mastered ordeal—and there will be nothing easy and pretty in that mark—but as Malraux reminds us, "always, however brutal an age may actually have been, its style transmits its music only."

I believe future generations will think of our times as the age of wholeness: when the walls began to fall; when the fragments began to be related to each other; when man learned finally to esteem tenderness and reason and awareness and the word which set him apart forever from other living creatures;

when he learned to realize his brokenness and his great talent for creating ties that bind him together again; when he learned to accept his own childhood and in the acceptance to become capable of maturity; when he began to realize his infinite possibilities even as he sees more clearly his limitations; when he began to see that sameness and normality are not relevant to human beings but to machines and animals; when he learned never to let any power or dictator cut his ties to the great reservoir of knowledge and wisdom without which he would quickly lose his human status; when he learned to live a bit more comfortably with time and space; when he learned to accept his need of God and the law that he cannot use Him, to accept his need of his fellow men and the law that he cannot use them, either; when he learned that "what is impenetrable to us really exists," and always there will be need of the dream, the belief, the wonder, the faith.

To believe in something not yet proved and to underwrite it with our lives: it is the only way we can leave the future open. Man, surrounded by facts, permitting himself no surmise, no intuitive flash, no great hypothesis, no risk is in a locked cell. Ignorance cannot seal the mind and imagination more surely. To find the point where hypothesis and fact meet; the delicate equilibrium between dream and reality; the place where fantasy and earthy things are metamorphosed into a work of art; the hour when faith in the future becomes knowledge of the past; to lay down one's power for others in need; to shake off the old ordeal and get ready for the new; to question, knowing that never can the full answer be found; to accept uncertainties quietly, even our incomplete knowledge of God: this is what man's journey is about, I think.